THE FREEMASONS

THE
FREEMASONS

THE ILLUSTRATED BOOK OF
AN ANCIENT BROTHERHOOD

MICHAEL JOHNSTONE

GRAMERCY BOOKS
NEW YORK

No part of this book may be reproduced or transmitted in
any form or by any means electronic or mechanical
including photocopying and recording, or by any
information storage and retrieval system, without
permission in writing from the publisher.

This 2005 edition is published by Gramercy Books, an
imprint of Random House Value Publishing, a division of
Random House, Inc., New York, by arrangement with
Arcturus Publishing Limited.

Gramercy is a registered trademark and the colophon is a
trademark of Random House, Inc.

Random House
New York • Toronto • London • Sydney • Auckland
www.randomhouse.com

Printed and bound in China

A catalog record for this title is available from the
Library of Congress.

ISBN 0-517-22666-9

10 9 8 7 6 5 4 3 2 1

Cover Design: Steve Flight
Art Director: Beatriz Waller
Design: Alex Ingr

*Title page: A 19th-century painted leather apron of a Master of
the Saint-Julien Lodge in Brioude, Le Puy-en-Velay (Musée Crozatier).*

CONTENTS

Introduction 7

In the Beginning 9

Built for the Glory of God 23

Emergence 42

Around the World 61

Crossing the Atlantic..................... 83

Rites and Rituals 101

Ideals and Virtues 118

Famous Freemasons 129

Women in Freemasonry 134

Glossary 138

Index 142

the Operative or Stone Masons

INTRODUCTION

Modern Freemasonry, often called 'The Craft' by modern Freemasons, can be said to have been founded in 1717 when the members of four or more old lodges met at the Apple Tree Tavern in London and agreed to constitute themselves as a Grand Lodge. The men decided to meet later, on June 24, St John the Baptist's Day, at another inn, The Goose and Gridiron, in St Paul's Churchyard to enjoy a feast and to choose a Grand Master from among their number. History does not record what fine fare the men enjoyed, but we do know that one Anthony Sayer 'gentleman' was elected Grand Master.

Since then, lodges have been founded in almost every country in the world and some of the most famous names in history have been proud to have been initiated into membership. The list is as long as it is diverse, Jonathan Swift, chronicler of *Gulliver's Travels* is believed to have been a member of Lodge Number 16, which met at The Goat, an inn on London's Haymarket. Benjamin Franklin and George Washington, two of the founding fathers of the United States, were members of St John's Lodge in Philadelphia and Frederickburg, Virginia respectively. Simon Bolivar 'The George Washington of South America' became a member of The Craft in Cadiz and in 1824 founded the Lodge Order and Liberty No. 2 in Peru. And Louis 'Satchmo' Armstrong was a member of Lodge Montgomery No.18 in New York. From 'Buzz' Aldrin, who was a footstep behind Neil Armstrong when the USA landed the first two men on the Moon in 1969, to John Zoffany, one of the founders of Britain's Royal Academy and a member of London's Lodge of Nine Muses, there are countless thousands of men who have been proud to have called themselves Freemasons.

Freemasonry has been banned in some places and flourished in others. Its members have played a significant part in major historical events, including the French Revolution and the founding of the United States of America. Its members are famous for their willingness to extend the hand of friendship to fellow Masons, regardless of class, colour or creed, or whichever Masonic tradition they follow.

As HRH the Duke of Kent, Grand Master of the United Kingdom of the United Grand Lodge of England has written, 'Each [lodge] developed in its own way with its own traditions and differences, but all subscribe to the same basic principles of Brotherly Love, Relief and Truth. Among [its members] have been some who were, and are, prominent in various areas of life and whose work and ideas have materially affected or greatly enriched the lives of not only their fellow members but mankind in general. Most of them, however, have been ordinary men who have attempted to live their lives by the practical lessons of morality, duty and service which they have learned in their lodges.'

And what could be a more fitting tribute to Freemasonry than that?

The George Washington Masonic Memorial, Virginia, which was dedicated to the memory of the first president on 12 May 1932 as an expression of the Masonic fraternity's faith in the principles of civil and religious liberty and orderly government

The Tower of Babel. According to York Rite Masonry, 'At the making of the Tower of Babel there was Masonry first much esteemed of...'

In the Beginning

Modern Freemasonry, established in London in 1717, claims that its origins date back thousands of years to pre-biblical times. According to legend, in the beginning . . .

There was a man called Lamech who had two sons by one wife, and a third son and a daughter by his second wife. These four children grew to adulthood and became the founders of all the crafts of the world. Jabal founded geometry. Jubal was music's progenitor. Tubal Cain was the first to take to the smithy. And his sister, whose name, alas, is not recorded, discovered the weaver's craft. The four were warned in dreams that man's sins had displeased God to such an extent that he was intent on wreaking his vengeance on them either by flame or flood.

RANULF HIGDEN'S HISTORY

At this point we shall let Ranulf Higden, a fourteenth-century monk who lived in Chester and is credited with being the author of *Polychronicon*, a history of the world, take up the story. Brother Ranulf learned the tale from a source quoting the words of the Greek historian Berosus, who was writing around 300BC. He had, in turn, copied from a Sumerian source of some 1,200 years earlier:

> *Wherefore they wrote these sciences which were found in two pillars of Stone that they might be found after the flood. The one stone was called marble that cannot burn with fire. The other was called Lateras that cannot drown with water. Our Intent is now to tell you truly how and in what manner these stones were found whereon these Crafts were written. The Greek Hermenes that was son unto Cus, and Cus was son unto Sem who was son unto Noah. This same Hermenes was afterwards called Hermes the father of wise men and he found out the two pillars of stone whereon the sciences were written and taught them forth. At the making of the Tower of Babylon [Babel] there was the craft of Masonry then first found and made much of and the king of Babylon who was called Hembroth or Nembroth was a mason and loved well the Craft.*

Higden goes on to describe how the king of Babylon passed on the knowledge contained in the Pillars to the sixty masons he sent to the city of Nineveh. From there it passed into Egypt where, centuries later, it was learned by Euclid, the Greek mathematician who lived in Alexandria. In response to a plea by the pharaoh, Euclid offered to teach the sons of wellborn Egyptians the science of geometry 'in practice to work masonry and all manner of worthy works that belonged to the building of castles and all manner of Courts Temples Churches with all other building'. Not only did Euclid teach his science to the Egyptians, he taught that they should be loyal to the pharaoh and to the lords whom they served. He also instructed that they should live well together and be true to one another, that they should call one another 'fellow and not servant or knave nor other foul names' and that they should 'truly serve for their payment the lord they served'.

As we shall see, these words are echoed 1,500 years after Euclid's time in the *Regius* manuscript (AD1390), which evokes the organization of masons and stone-

King Solomon's Temple in Jerusalem. While it was being built Hiram-Abiff was attacked and murdered, an event that continues to be remembered in present-day Freemasonry

cutters in medieval England, and in the Statute of Ratisbon, which did the same for German masons 70 years later.

The good monk Ranulf Higden of Chester also records the building of the Temple in Jerusalem. He writes that long after the Children of Israel came into the land that we now Israel, King David ordered that a new temple be built in the city of Jerusalem. When David died, Solomon 'son unto David' set about completing the work that his father had begun.

Solomon looked abroad for assistance to help him finish the Temple. Among the countries Solomon asked for help was neighbouring Tyre, whose ruler, King Hiram, agreed to furnish him with timber from the cedar forests of Lebanon. Hiram also agreed to send his best architects, who had learned the mason's craft from the heirs of the children of Lamech, to help in the construction of the Temple.

According to some accounts, Hiram sent his son, Aynon, who was skilled in the science of geometry, to Jerusalem, where Solomon made him master of all the other masons. But it is more commonly believed that it was a brass-worker's son, Hiram-Abiff, whom Hiram sent, along with the materials Solomon had asked for. The fact that Abiff means 'son of' and the king and the brass-worker shared the same name contributes to the confusion about who it was who went to Solomon's assistance.

Whichever it is, the legend has it that because the Tyrean master mason spoke a different language to his workers, a system of special words, signs and touches evolved to help him communicate with the artisans and fellow masons. Some of

10

these signs and symbols are thought to be the same as those that feature in modern Masonic ceremony.

Hiram-Abiff's workers were divided into three groups: apprentices, companions and masters. On days when they were due to be paid, they presented themselves to the Temple with a password given to them by Hiram-Abiff, without which they would not be paid. There were countless thousands of workers, and the paymasters could hardly have been expected to recognize which were the genuine claimants. The apprentices met around Jachim, one of the two 12 metre-tall pillars that had been erected in front of the entrance, and the companions around Boaz, the second of the pillars. The masters assembled in the central room of the Temple.

The story goes that there were three ne'er-do-wells among Hiram-Abiff's workforce. (Given the number of men working on the Temple, it is surprising that there were only three!) The trio were named Jebulas, a mason, Jubelos, a carpenter, and a general craftsman called Jebulem. They wanted promotion to the rank of Master and the high salary that went with the office, but they did not want to go through the various stages required to achieve it. Planning to force Hiram-Abiff into promoting them, they each took a place at one of the three doors of the Temple and waited for him. When Hiram-Abiff came to the South Gate, Jubelos made his demand, which was refused. Angered by this, Jubelos went to hit the Tyrean on the throat with his ruler, but he missed and struck him on the shoulder instead. Hiram-Abiff ran to the West Gate where Jubelas was waiting. When he also was turned down for promotion, he struck Hiram on the left of the chest with his iron square. Hiram sped towards the East Gate where the same scene was replayed, only this time the waiting mason hit out with his mallet, killing Hiram-Abiff on the spot.

The tools of the crime and the parts of the body they hit have great symbolism for Freemasons. The ruler stands for precision, the square for rectitude and the mallet for will. The first assailant went for the throat, seat of material life; the second for the heart, seat of the soul; and the third for the forehead, seat of intelligence. And the three assassins are symbolic of the three banes of life – untruth, ignorance and ambition or Inner Darkness. Hiram-Abiff himself stands for the Light.

Hiram-Abiff died having, in Higden's words, 'confirmed the worthy craft of masons in the Country of Jerusalem . . . and in many other kingdoms glorious craftsmen walking abroad in diverse countries, some because of learning more craft and others some to teach their craft'.

A MAN OF MANY TALENTS

Another man who, some historians believe, may have a link with the origins of Freemasonry and its rituals is the great Greek philosopher Pythagoras, who was born at Samos in the sixth century BC. After immersing himself in Greek culture from an early age, from which he was taught that the earth sat at the centre of the universe, with the sun and the planets revolving around it, he travelled to Memphis in Egypt. He stayed there for many years and learned about numbers, symbols, geometry, astronomy and the mysteries of Egyptian religion. In Memphis, he came to believe in the reincarnation of the soul, it being a portion of the great universal soul, to which we return when we die.

Shortly after completing his training at Memphis, Egypt was invaded by the Persians. Pythagoras, along with other scholars and priests, was taken to Babylon, where he was held captive for 12 years. Although he was 'a prisoner', he was free to mix with scholars of different religions and beliefs. There were men who taught monotheism or belief in one god, and others who preached the Persian belief in dualism, which held that reality consists of two basic types of substance, mind and matter, or two basic types of entity, mental and physical. Pythagoras met Hindu philosophers and Zoroastrians, whose belief that Ormuzd, the creator and Angel of Good, would triumph over the evil Ahriman was central to their occultism. It is no wonder that Pythagoras is regarded as a man of very deep learning in mysticism.

When he was eventually given his freedom, Pythagoras settled first in Delphi in Greece and later in Crotone on the Italian coast, where he founded a school of eso-

Pythagoras, the Ancient Greek philosopher and mathematician who established an academy, which some believe is one of the wells from which the Craft sprung

teric philosophy. A statue of Hermes, the keeper of esoteric knowledge according to Greek philosophy, stood at the gate of the school, warning the layman to stand back. Would-be pupils underwent a brief trial period of a few months before becoming novices. At the end of the trial period, the aspirant was put to the test physically and morally.

One trial was to survive a night alone in a pitch-black cavern reputed to be haunted by the ghosts of failed candidates or men who had betrayed the school's ideals, who appeared in terrifying apparitions. Those who passed this test were then locked in a bare cell for a week with just a crust of bread and a pitcher of water on which to survive. They were also given a board on which they were expected to write the meaning of Pythagorean symbols. That done, the candidate was then led into a large room where he was harangued and mocked, and harassed with difficult questions, the answers to which he was expected to have at the ready. Failure was met with instant dismissal from the school; success with promotion to novice.

For three years the novices were immersed in Pythagorean philosophy, which was founded on the principles of respect, tolerance and the union of religion and people in general. Mornings were devoted to lessons, afternoons to physical exercise, and evenings to prayer, lectures and discussion.

Novices were taught that parents were the earthly representatives of the deities and were to be respected as such. Marriage was regarded as a sacred institution and wives were to be treated as equals, which was something rare in classical times. A friend was seen as an alter ego and was to be accorded similar respect to parents. Suffering was considered as the anvil on which the human soul was forged, and although it was to be endured bravely, it was never to be deliberately caused.

The novice period completed, the disciple was allowed to enter the Inner Court where he was initiated into the 'Sacred Word', the Pythagorean science of numbers, which many regard as giving a direct link with Freemasonry and its signs and symbols.

1 (point)
Indivisible, infinite, and the root of all things is God.

2 (line)
Man and woman united in the One God.

3 (triangle)
The perfect number. Three elements – spirit, soul and body –
make up man. Three ideals – wisdom, strength and beauty.

4 (square)
Represents the four directions and is the key bearer of nature.

5 (pentagram)
Stands for free will and justice, as well as strife.

6 (hexagram)
Shows the six directions of space. According to Pythagoras
it shows the harmonious perfection of parts.

7 (triangle and square)
A pure and perfect number. The symbol of life, it unites the four
elements of the body with the three elements of the soul.

8 (two squares)
Is the number of Universal Harmony and makes love and
friendship one.

9 (three triangles)
The number of the Muses in Greek mythology, the daughters of Zeus
and Mnemosyne, who are each identified with their own art or
science and therefore represents the knowledge of science and art.

10 (tetractys)
The source of counting and stands for the World, for Fate and
for Eternity.

Knowledge of 'the Sacred Word' acquired, the disciple was then immersed in Science, which was taught either at night or by the sea. And when this, the 'Third Degree of Initiation', had been achieved, the Fourth was aspired to, at which point the disciple was expected to demonstrate clairvoyant abilities.

Now an adept, the disciple left the school. If anyone was thought to have betrayed its secrets, a tomb was erected in his name and his soul was pronounced dead, something that bears a strong resemblance to the old Masonic practice of symbolically burning on a pyre anyone who betrays The Craft's secrets.

TRIBAL ROOTS?

Another theory concerning the origins of Masonry is that it has roots with tribes that flourished in Megalithic times from around 7,000BC to 2,500BC. Having discovered science and astronomy, men of that age built astronomical observatories, which include England's Stonehenge on the edge of Salisbury Plain, that were astonishing achievements for those times. Such sites enabled the tribes who built them to chart the seasons and years by observing the sun and Venus, the brightest planet in the night sky. In effect this allowed them to keep track of time. Without timekeeping, early civilisations would have been quite unable to plan for the future or progress towards it efficiently.

One of the Dead Sea Scrolls, discovered in caves in the Middle East close to the sea that gives them their name between 1947 and 1958, and which are thought to have been written between 100BC and AD68, is the *Book of Enoch*. It explains the scientific principles by which these early observatories operated. These principles were shared with other tribes prior to a devastating flood that hit the world in around 150BC.

The survivors continued the traditions, and when the Romans expelled their priests from Jerusalem in AD70 they hid scrolls, on which they had written their knowledge of stonemasonry, in the ruins of Solomon's Temple. There they lay until they were recovered by their descendants, the men who founded the Knights Templa (see page 17). Led by Hugues de Payens in 1140, a group of Templars retrieved the scrolls and took them to Europe. There the secret skills of the stonemasons of Old Testament times were passed on to the men who used them to create the great cathedrals of Europe, the men whose rituals, organizations, symbols and signs are so evident in modern Freemasonry.

OF MYSTERIES AND MASTERS

Fact or fiction? The truth is that we shall never know. But what we can safely say is that the roots of Freemasonry are as old as organized building itself. For when men and women first learned to cut stone, when rulers decided to use that stone to erect temples to their gods and shrines to their vanity, when men learned the craft of masonry, that is when the seeds of Freemasonry were sown.

Thousands of years after that, during the Middle Ages and the great era of Christian cathedral building, the masons and other craftsmen re-emerged from the shadows of history to work in York, Chartres, Cologne, and in Paris and other cities

Mithras, sacred to the Ancient Persians, in whose symbolic rituals some detect a link with The Craft

renowned for the masterpieces of medieval ecclesiastical architecture they boast.

Because it is from the organization, customs and practices of these medieval masons that modern Freemasonry claims its inheritance, many historians have asked if there was any one body to whom the ancient masons entrusted their secrets until their skills were to be needed again. Is there, they have asked, one direct ancestor of today's Freemasonry? The brief A–Z of some of them that follows serves simply to give an idea of how many and varied they are, for if truth be told, we will never know.

THE ANCIENT MYSTERIES

The ancients of Greece and Egypt, and the Persians who worshipped Mithras, the god of light in the Persian pantheon, used symbolism to teach mortality and devise elaborate rituals which some see as a direct link to The Craft. But from what we know, the differences between the ancient Mysteries and Freemasonry are more pronounced than any similarities. What similarities there are could well have developed at different times and in different places quite independently of each other.

BOX CLUB CHARITIES

A recent theory holds that modern Freemasonry evolved from charitable beginnings rather than the masons of medieval times. During the early seventeenth century, many trades operated what became known as 'box clubs'. Members of these clubs would set aside a small portion of their earnings to be used by the group when hard times fell, or by individual members who found themselves in distressing poverty. Even the smallest sum of money often stood between life and death for those in dire straits and suffering from starvation. There is evidence that the box clubs began to admit members from outside their trade and acquired the characteristics of early Masonic lodges. Freemasonry, some believe, arose from the network of these clubs, which was taken over by intellectuals later in the century.

THE COLLEGIA

The Collegia is one of the bodies of architects or builders that could have handed down the moral teachings and symbolism that came into the possession of medieval masons and eventually flourished into The Craft. It combined religious, social and craft aspects. When the Roman Empire was at its height, the authorities encouraged the Collegia in its operations. Some students of Freemasonry believe that members of the Collegia were principally craftsmen builders who either travelled with the Roman army when it invaded the British Isles or followed it when much of what became England had come firmly under Roman control, which was by the middle of the first century AD.

Three or four hundred years later, when the Romans withdrew to mainland Europe, some of the Collegia stayed behind to ensure that their skills not only survived but were passed on. These skills were passed down through the generations to the Anglo-Saxon craftsmen whose skills were put to use during the Middle Ages.

This argument is countered by those who point to the fact that there is no evidence that members of the Collegia were teachers. They also say that at least 500 years elapsed between the time when the Romans quit Britain and the very first evidence of the existence of craft-based organizations among masons in the early Middle Ages.

THE COMACINE MASTERS

Taking their name from Lake Como in northern Italy, where they had their original headquarters, the Comacine Masters were a body of Lombard builders who were influential in the development and spread of Romanesque architecture. This style was widely adopted in western and southern Europe from the ninth to the twelfth centuries and was characterized by rounded arches and massive masonry wall construction. The Comacines were in great demand in western Europe, but it is doubtful if they ever organized themselves into a unified body. Even if they had done so, there is nothing to suggest that they used the symbols, secret signs and words that would point to their being in any way a direct link to the Freemasons.

THE COMPAGNONNAGE

Craft guilds appeared in France before they were first noted in England and Germany. An organization of masons was in existence in France as early as 1365, and a code governing their practices dating from 1407 can be found in the archives of the city of Amiens. There is mention of an earlier code dating from 1260 which refers to Charles Martel, grandfather of Charlemagne and one of the men to whom the secrets of the ancient masons are said to have been passed.

But it is another French organization that has excited the attention of those who seek Freemasonry's true ancestor: the Compagnonnage.

In 1841 a French historian, Agricol Perdiguer, published the *Livre du Compagnonnage*, which gives a detailed account of a mysterious organization of masons which, according to the book, was composed of the Sons of Solomon, the Sons of Soubise

Charles Martel, the eighth-century French ruler and grandfather of Charlemagne. Members of the Compagnonnage believe he came to hold the secrets of King Solomon's masons

and the Sons of Maître Jacques. French legend has it that this Maître Jacques was one of the master masons who worked on Solomon's Temple and was a colleague of Hiram-Abiff, the Tyrean master mason who was sent to Jerusalem to help build the Temple.

Perdiguer writes that on completion of their apprenticeships and their acceptance in 'the company' journeymen masons were expected to travel round France and beyond its borders looking for work. A code of practice was established whereby the journeymen were to be given suitable work when they asked for it and assistance to help them on their way. Many of the ceremonies that Perdiguer describes are similar to those that feature in English Freemasonry. However, as the book was not published until over a century after the Grand Lodge had been founded in London, it could well be that the author had used knowledge of its ritual to describe that of the Compagnonnage.

Also, in England the rituals of the masons were adopted by the Freemasons: in France, the Compagnonnage has remained separate from the established Craft there. Putting these two facts together, the Compagnonnage is unlikely to have been the direct progenitor of Freemasonry.

DRUIDS

Druidism was widely practised in the British Isles more than 2,000 years ago, before it was driven underground by the Roman conquerors. The Druids seem to have combined the functions of priests, judges and politicians, holding their rites in sacred oak groves, where human sacrifices may well have been offered to whichever deities the priests worshipped. In the eighteenth and nineteenth centuries there was a revival of interest in Druidism, but our knowledge of the original beliefs and ceremonies is at best sketchy. If there is a link with Freemasonry, it is lost in the mists of time.

THE ESSENES

The members of this Jewish fraternity that originated in the second century BC lived a monastic life in the region of the Dead Sea in Israel. Unlike followers of many other contemporary religions, they rejected animal sacrifice as a means of pleasing their god. They were celebrated for their piety, virtue and strict observance of the Sabbath. The Essenes were more or less self-sufficient, maintaining themselves with manual labour, and were generous with their charity to others. They lived in fellowship with one another and held that what was owned by one was owned by all.

THE KNIGHTS TEMPLAR

Perhaps the most romantic of the suggested ancestors of Freemasonry, and certainly the one about which most has been written, are the Knights Templar. The order was established in 1118 by Hugues (or Hugh) de Payens and eight other French knights, who set themselves up to protect pilgrims journeying from the port of Jaffra to Jerusalem in the Holy Land. The Knights took monastic vows and set up their headquarters on the site of Solomon's Temple in Jerusalem, hence their name.

They wore long white robes decorated with a red cross on the left shoulder and their seal was witness to their bonds of brotherhood – two knights riding one horse. Members of the Order gained a reputation for bravery in battle and became known for the houses which offered hospitality to pilgrims as they travelled to and from Jerusalem.

They were eventually expelled from Jerusalem after the fall of Acre in 1291, and later the order was suppressed, mainly on account of jealousy of its wealth and power. In London, their headquarters was on the site that is still called the Temple, close to Holborn where they had their first house. It is now two of the city's Inns of Court – Inner Temple and Outer Temple – two of London's legal centres. In France,

A medieval Knight Templar wearing house robes. The Knights Templar continue to play an important part in Scottish and York Rite Freemasonry

Dating from the fifteenth century, Rosslyn Chapel and the Prentice Pillar have strong associations with the Knights Templar and modern Freemasonry

where the Order was suppressed with particular cruelty, their stronghold was taken over by the Knights of St John. The old tower of the building later became the prison where Louis XVI and his family were incarcerated prior to his execution and that of his queen, Marie Antoinette, in 1793.

During the years in which the Knights flourished, its members employed masons to work in their temples and in the grand houses many of them built for themselves. According to some historians of The Craft, it is likely that they shared some of their knowledge and rituals with the senior stone masons they employed and that these master craftsmen later incorporated the knowledge and the rituals they had learned from the Templars into their own traditions.

For the first few years of their existence there were too few knights to offer effective escort to the pilgrims. We know, thanks to evidence found by Lieutenant Warren of the Royal Engineers in 1867, that during their first decade of existence they excavated the ruins of Solomon's Temple. Legend has it that they unearthed something of huge spiritual or material value. Certainly they became immensely rich, almost overnight in historical terms. Could, some have asked, the secrets of Solomon's masons have been among whatever the Templars unearthed?

To return to France, in 1305, King Philip IV, being on the verge of bankruptcy, confiscated the lands and possessions of French Jews. Two years later, having quickly squandered what he stole, Philip decided to do the same thing to the Templars. Not satisfied with requisitioning their lands and possessions, he was later given papal authority to instruct the Inquisition to torture information out of any captured Templars that would legitimize what has been described as 'grand larceny'. Philip's sobriquet, 'the Fair' was obviously an allusion to his appearance rather than to his treatment of many of his subjects!

Many Templars managed to get themselves, their families, and at least some of their wealth, out of the country and it is from this exodus from France to other parts of Europe, and in particular Scotland, that the fount of much Freemasonic folklore springs.

At the time of the Order's suppression in France Scotland was ruled by Robert the Bruce, a man who had been excommunicated by the Catholic Church. There, beyond the jurisdiction of the pope and the Catholic Church's Inquisition, the exiled Templars were comparatively safe. Many scholars of The Craft believe the Templars required a degree of privacy from church and state, even in comparatively liberal Scotland, where guilds of masons had already been established. The Templars would have found the stone masons' guilds attractive organizations to infiltrate, given the secrecy under which they operated. In return, some historians believe, they passed to guild members the secrets of Templar rites and symbols, which became the rites and symbols of Freemasonry when the masons' craft lodges evolved into The Craft.

To back up their theory, these scholars point to Rosslyn Chapel, which is situated in a village eight kilometres south of Scotland's capital, Edinburgh. Rosslyn has always been steeped in mystery to locals and visitors alike, the number of which has increased hugely since 2003, featuring as it does in the best-selling novel, *The Da Vinci Code*. The chapel, which took 40 years to build, was commissioned by Sir William St Clair, whose family is said to have been descended from Hugues de Payens, founder of the Templars.

That may or may not be true, but what is known is that the chapel was constructed at a time when books were subject to censorship. This, and the fact the chapel walls are embellished with Templar and perhaps Masonic symbols and imagery, has led some scholars to believe that when Sir William instructed his craftsmen, he did so with the express intention of leaving permanent and curious encoded messages in the chapel's fabric. The carving surrounding the ground floor south-west window, for example, depicts a Templar initiation ceremony, which appears to have much in common with Freemasonry ritual. The eastern end of the

Philip IV of France had little difficulty in persuading Pope Clement V to allow torture of the Knights Templar

chapel features unusual pillars which recall Wisdom, Strength and Beauty – three of the most powerful symbols of Freemasonry, representing as they do God's omniscience and omnipotence, and the symmetry and order of His creation.

But it is what has become known as the 'Prentice Pillar' that has excited most interest among those seeking a connection between Freemasonry and the Knights Templar.

Standing in the south of the chapel, this striking and ornate pillar spirals upward from the eight dragons that curve round its base. One legend has it that the master mason who had intended to carve it travelled to Rome, carrying the plans for the proposed design with him. When he returned, he found that not only had the work been done for him by his apprentice, but that it had been done with such exquisite craftsmanship that the jealous master struck his pupil down and killed him. But those looking for links with Freemasonry claim another version of the origins of the pillar. In the book *The Hiram Key* it is suggested that the pillar, together with a head carved elsewhere in the chapel and displaying a gash in the forehead, recalls Hiram-Abiff, who was killed by jealous ne'er-do-wells while working on King Solomon's temple in Jerusalem.

The connection between the chapel and stonemasons' guilds (and hence, perhaps, Freemasonry) is strengthened by a reference in the official guidebook to a descendant of the chapel's founder being granted the Charters of 1630 by the Masons of Scotland. The Charters recognized that the position of Grand Master Mason of Scotland had been hereditary in the St Clair family since 1441, when it was granted by James II, the original charter having been destroyed in a fire.

In November 1736, when the Grand Lodge of Scotland was formed, Sir William Sinclair became Grand Master, but he was obliged by his fellow members to sign a declaration as head of the family at Rosslyn, resigning in perpetuity the Sinclair family's heredity patronage of the Scottish Craft.

As with so much of The Craft's history, we shall never know for sure. If there is a link between the Knights Templar and modern Freemasonry, it may be at best direct, at least tenuous, or at worst mere myth! But what has to be said is that the Templar connection lends romance and colour to the history of The Craft.

THE ROSICRUCIANS

From the late Middle Ages, men known as Kabbalists were widely concerned with concocting and deciphering charms and anagrams and in searching for the philosopher's stone that would turn base metal into gold. This particular cabbalistic group was first heard of in 1614 when a manuscript, *Fama fraternitatis des loblichen Ordens des Rosenkreuzes (The Universal and General Reformation of the Whole Wide World by the Order of Rosenkrantz)* was published in Kassel in Germany's Rhineland.

The manuscript described how some years before the grave of a mythical character called Christian Rosenkrantz had been stumbled upon deep in thick forest. Beside the tomb was a small table on which lay three books that Rosenkrantz had written. Their author claimed to have been born in 1384 and still to have been living in 1490 at the ripe (and unprecedented) old age of 106. He had spent much of his life travelling in the east and learning various philosophies there. Rosenkrantz wrote about a time when man would be at one with the 'Supreme Being' who had no truck with religious differences and who granted religious toleration for all. More than one expert has pointed out that even if the Rosicrucians did exist at the beginning of the seventeenth century, the Masonic lodges that were to evolve into Freemasonry were already widely distributed in the British Isles, particularly in Scotland.

TRAVELLING ARCHITECTS

In one of his diaries, John Aubrey, a contemporary of Samuel Pepys and like him a chronicler of his times, records a remark made by a fellow antiquarian that around the time of Henry III (1207–72) the pope authorized a 'Company of Italian Architects' to travel across Europe to build churches. Aubrey writes that, according to his source, 'from these are derived the Fraternity of Freemasons'. Unfortunately, searches of the Vatican archives have so far failed to unearth any documentary evidence to support this theory, and, also, although masons may have been mainly occupied in church building, they were never exclusively so. As extremely skilled free agents, they would work for whoever had the money to pay them, churchman or layman alike.

UNANSWERED QUESTIONS

Did King Solomon 'send unto Tyre' for help in building his great Temple in Jerusalem? Were the secrets of King Hiram's builders passed on to one brotherhood or another to be guarded until they were needed by some future generation of masons? Are today's Freemasons the heirs of these Biblical builders? Maybe buried deep in the desert sand lies a stone tablet whose markings could tell us the truth. Perhaps in some great library there is an ancient scroll or manuscript that lays out the facts. Until one or the other is unearthed we have no alternative other than to accept the fact that the origins of pre-modern Freemasonry are lost in the dim and distant past. They are shrouded in a cloak of mystery, and it is entirely probable that the cloak will never be fully unfolded.

An example of Rosicrucian art. The Rosicrucians cloaked their ideas in mysticism and symbolism which is recalled in modern Freemasonry in the Rose Croix degree of the Ancient and Accepted Scottish Rite

Countless men spent their entire working lives labouring at the Notre Dame Cathedral in Paris. Many would have started as apprentices, working their way up to Master Mason

BUILT FOR THE GLORY OF GOD

With their roots stretching back across the millennia, the masons can rightly claim to be the heirs of some of the greatest craftsmen the world has ever seen. . .

From the third to the ninth century AD and beyond, when the Mayan culture was flourishing in Central America, Europe was plunged into what historians called the Dark Ages. Academics date the end of this time from 1137, when the discovery of the ancient treatises in Italy, known as the Pandects of Amalfi sparked a renewal in learning and culture in Europe. Much of this renewal was sponsored, if not directly by the Roman Catholic Church, then by wealthy noblemen keen to find favour in the eyes of the Lord (and the patronage at the disposal of the pope and other powerful churchmen). Among the legacies they left us are the Romanesque and Gothic cathedrals of Catholic Europe. Built to the glory of God in the Highest (and perhaps to satisfy man's conceit of himself as the pinnacle of God's creation), they could collectively lay claim to being one of the wonders of the modern world.

CLASSICAL INSPIRATIONS

Early cathedral builders took their inspiration from the buildings of classical Greece and Rome. Gradually, the Romanesque style developed with architects basing their designs on the cross-shaped ground plans of early Christian churches. Flying buttresses evolved in the twelfth century and came to be widely used along with the pointed arches, decorative gables, delicate tracery and majestic stained-glass windows that typify the Gothic style, which was brought to awe-inspiring maturity in Salisbury's Cathedral and Paris' Notre Dame.

As the centuries unfolded, in cities all over Europe generations of men toiled to design and build magnificent cathedrals and lesser, but equally ornate, churches. It took decades, centuries even, to transform architects' plans into finished buildings. Glassmakers created the luminescent stained-glass windows that beautify so many cathedrals. Woodcarvers fashioned ornate altars and screens. Sculptors hewed votive figures out of blocks of marble. And some of the most skilled artists the world has ever known were commissioned to paint biblical scenes on altarpieces and shrines.

FIRST AMONG EQUALS

But the architects' plans had to be turned to stone buildings before the skills of these and other craftsmen could be put to use. Someone had to build the walls, the pillars, the steeples and dreaming spires that led the eye heavenwards. That 'someone' was the mason – the stonecutters and builders who translated the abstract of the architects' plans into the reality of the buildings that even today – six, seven, eight centuries later – act as a magnet to worshippers and tourists alike.

23

Secret Places

These men had to have somewhere to arrange and store their tools; a place where master builders could give orders to more junior craftsmen and apprentices. They needed somewhere to shelter when bad weather made work impossible, and a place where, if work was suspended for any length of time, the mason's skills could be taught to apprentices.

Known as a *Hutte, lutza, cassina* or *loge,* depending on location, they are known to us as 'lodges', and almost every cathedral building site in medieval Europe had one; if it was not against the outer wall of the cathedral, it would only be a few steps from it at most. Built of wood or stone, the lodges came to be seen as a place in which the techniques and secrets of the masons' craft were passed on. This training could not be given where it could be seen or heard by non-lodge members, and so the lodge came to be regarded as a protected place and in time assumed a sacred character.

With so much cathedral building occuring all over Europe, countless lodges came into being. They were usually dissolved on the completion of the building work, but as construction could take several life spans, the lodges lasted for generations. Customs and rules differed from one lodge to the other, and it was not until 1459 that an attempt was made to unify the various codes and statutes of the masons' lodges of Europe's cathedral builders.

The Ratisbon Statutes

In 1459 stonemasons from all over Europe gathered in the city of Ratisbon (modern Regensburg) in western Germany under the presidency of Jost Dotzinger, master of works of Strasbourg Cathedral. Their aim was to standardize the statutes of their respective lodges. The result was the Statutes of Ratisbon, which describe in great detail the organization and daily life of the lodges, which were placed under the authority of the four main lodges – Strasbourg, Cologne, Vienna and Rome. Strasbourg was given the rank of Grand Lodge and its decision was final in the event of any dispute.

The lodges of the English and Scottish masons were not affected by the Statutes of Ratisbon. They had their own rules, formulated at a meeting presided over by King Athelstane towards the end of the ninth century and contained in a royal charter (see p 31).

The Ratisbon Statutes were eventually given royal approval in 1498 when the Emperor Maximilian recognized them. Seventy years or so later, they were revised in a text that was of equal importance in its approach to the organization and regulations in force in the communities of builders. This revision was contained in the Statutes of St Michael.

After a short preamble, the Ratisbon Statutes, which had to be read to members of the lodges once a year, begin by demanding that whoever wished to join a fraternal organization must promise to abide by all the points and articles covered. They then go on to cover the responsibilities of the master and the duties of those who work for him. For example, if a master undertook another project concurrent with one on which he was already working and was unable to complete it successfully so that another master took it up, it was the latter's responsibility to ensure that the work was completed on time. And if a master took up work for which he was not competent, he was forbidden assistance.

Under the terms of the statutes, it was forbidden for a master to live openly with a woman who was not his wife. If anyone who broke this rule refused to mend his ways, 'no companion or stone-cutter should remain in his building site or have anything to do with him'.

It was the master's responsibility to ensure that each member of his lodge must 'drop one pfenning' into a chest in which fines and any other donations were saved to be handed over to the main lodge once a year.

Members had to receive Holy Communion once a year (not too arduous a responsibility at a time when the majority of the people in Europe went to mass at

least once a week) and were forbidden to gamble. Anyone admitted to a lodge who was found to be in breach of either of these rules was denied the fellowship of the lodge until he mended his ways and had taken whatever punishment he was given by the community.

The master to whom the books of a lodge were entrusted had to promise to look after them and not to let anyone copy them, except for one or two articles at most. Anyone who copied from the books without the knowledge of the master was expelled from the community, and hence from working, until he had made 'honourable amends'.

Members were barred from charging for teaching their skills to others in the corporation, but were encouraged to pass on their skills to their fellows for no payment as long as they were members. Non-members were refused even the most basic training.

However, non-members were allowed to take part in any religious observances, indeed, they were to be welcomed provided they paid an initial fee, followed by an annual due. However, apart from attending divine services they were forbidden to participate in the work of the corporation.

The statute was signed in grandiose style by Jost Dotziger, the Master of Works of Strasbourg Cathedral: 'In the year 1459, four weeks before Easter, the masters and the workers of this corporation who have come to Ratisbon, have sworn loyalty to the book.'

A depiction of Christ offering the Eucharist. It is set out in the Ratisbon Statutes that lodge members must take Mass at least once a year

Saint Barbara is patron saint of masons and stonecutters, so will have provided comfort to many Freemasons over the centuries (see p 28)

Later, the Grand Lodge of Stonecutters of Strasbourg issued decrees and articles that covered the behaviour and treatment of travelling companions or journeymen, who were guaranteed that if they moved on to another building site, but only after having completed their work satisfactorily on another, they should receive the same pay. They were forbidden to speak ill of their employer but had the right to denounce one whom they suspected of infringing the lodge rules. When they moved on, they were not to leave any debt behind or any cause for complaint.

Any employer who wanted to release a journeyman could only do so on a Saturday or on the evening of payday. This was to enable him to travel the next day.

If a companion (or a master) fell ill and was unable to provide for his needs, the corporation was duty bound to support him and lend him money, which was to be repaid as soon as possible. If he died in debt, his clothes and other possessions were to be seized and sold until what had been owed was recovered.

The rules governing apprentices were strict but fair. The youngsters had to be of legitimate birth and married. (It was not unusual for young teenagers to be wed in the Middle Ages: Romeo was sixteen and his Juliet two years younger when they knelt before Friar Lawrence to plight their troth.) Their apprenticeship had to last for a minimum for six years, but they could not be promoted to foreman until they had completed one year as a journeyman. They were sworn to respect the terms and rules of the corporation, but had the right, if they considered that their master had behaved badly or treated them unfairly, to bring their case to other members of the corporation. If their claim was not upheld, they could be asked to leave the corporation and seek work elsewhere.

And like companions, journeymen and masters, an apprentice who infringed the rules had to accept his punishment, and if they refused to do so, they were excluded from the corporation, 'avoided and despised by all', until the punishment had been fulfilled.

THE STATUTES OF ST MICHAEL

The revision known as the Statutes of St Michael revisited much of the same territory, and between them the two statutes give us a vital insight into what life was like in the lodges of the masons of medieval Europe. That said, it should not be assumed that there was a single order of stonemasons throughout Europe. The statutes do reveal a system that was highly hierarchical and that solemnly proclaimed fundamental values – fraternity, honesty, maintenance and preservation of trade secrets, being faithful to one's oath and professional and moral duties at all levels of the craft, professional training and last, but by no means least, prayer.

LIFE IN THE LODGES

Before looking at life in the lodges, it should be pointed out that modern Freemasonry borrows the symbols and vocabulary of the medieval masons and stonecutters, although they themselves do not practise their craft. The real inheritors of the cathedral builder's lodges are the French *cayennes* of the Companions of the Tour of France, whose true function is transmitting the techniques and knowledge to others within a professional brotherhood. That said, in contemporary Freemasonry the term 'lodge' and the manuscripts and other Middle Age statutes that regulated the organization of the masons and stonecutters are sanctified, albeit for symbolic rather than historical purposes.

Even before the statutes were written, the three main titles – Master, Companion and Apprentice – were used in the lodges. The Master was nominated to be head of the lodge, and it was his job to apply the statutes and see to it that all the members respected all the customs. The Master was a man of power whose duty it was to teach his art for no fee. He had his reserved place in the east end of the meeting room, a place no one else would dare to occupy.

A bell regulated the lodge's working day, which lasted from daybreak until sunset. There was a break for lunch, usually an hour, and a break for a drink in the afternoon. (In summer, when it was hot, two breaks of thirty minutes each were allowed.) During the winter, when the laying of stones was stopped because of the risk of ice and frost, the columns that had been begun were covered with straw and dung to protect them from the bad weather. Lodge members who had no work on site went to the quarry or perhaps returned to the land.

Workers were paid more in summer than in winter, when wages were cut by a third. Work was forbidden on Sundays and on holy days. One of the holiest to the Steinmetzen of Germany was November 8, the commemorative day of the Four Crowned Martyrs, the patron saints of the building trade. In truth, there were nine martyrs – five masons and four Roman soldiers – but they have come collectively to be known as *Quatour Coronati.* The name survives in Freemasonry. One London lodge, No. 2076, a German one in Bayreuth and another in Rome have adopted the name.

The masons – Claudius, Castorius, Nicostratus, Simphorianus and Simplicius – were Christians and highly skilled masons in the time of the emperor Diocletian (AD245–313). They refused to fashion a statue to Aesculapius, one of the gods worshipped by the citizens of Rome, so the furious emperor ordered that they be locked alive in lead coffins and cast into the River Tiber. Forty-two days later a fellow Christian, Nicodemus, recovered the coffins. During this time, other craftsmen had done Diocletian's bidding and worked on the statue. When it was finished, the emperor ordered the city militia to burn incense as an offering to the gods. Four Christian soldiers refused to take part in the ceremony and were scourged to death. Their bodies were then thrown to the dogs, but were rescued by fellow Christians and given Christian burial along with the five masons. The masons were martyred in AD298 and the soldiers two years later.

Melchiades (Pope between AD310 and AD314) had their relics removed from where they lay and put in a specially built basilica on the Caelian Hill. The basilica was dedicated to the Four Crowned Ones (the soldiers) and the Five Sculptor Martyrs. Almost from the very beginning, the citizens of Rome dropped mention of the Five Sculptor Martyrs (not through any lack of respect, but simply because the other five were assumed to be included when they talked of the Four Crowned Ones) and the masons became one with the military as the Four Crowned Martyrs.

The basilica was rebuilt by Pope Honorius in 622, three years after a church dedicated to the men had been erected in Canterbury. The Church of the Four Crowned Martyrs has long since gone, but it probably stood on the site where St Alphege's Church now sits.

The Martyrs are mentioned in the *Regius Manuscript* (see p. 31):

> *As did these holy martyrs four,*
> *That in this craft were of great honour;*
> *They were as good masons as on earth shall go,*
> *Gravers and image-makers they were also.*

The Four Crowned Martyrs are still revered today by masons whose arts were designated in medieval Germany and Italy *ars quatoue coronatorum* (the Art of the Four Crowned Men). Another patron saint of masons and stonecutters is Saint Barbara, who achieved her status having been imprisoned, and later killed, by her father for her beliefs.

TOWARDS BROTHERHOOD

We cannot estimate how many masons were at work during the age when the great cathedrals of Europe were under construction. In France alone in the early Middle Ages, from 1050 to 1350, more stone was quarried for eighty cathedrals than was used in Egypt during the millennia when the pyramids were built. And it was not just on cathedral sites that masons were employed. By the end of the Middle Ages it has been estimated that there was church for every two hundred inhabitants.

The men who worked on the early stages of church building were well aware that they were unlikely to see the building finished in their lifetimes, indeed in the

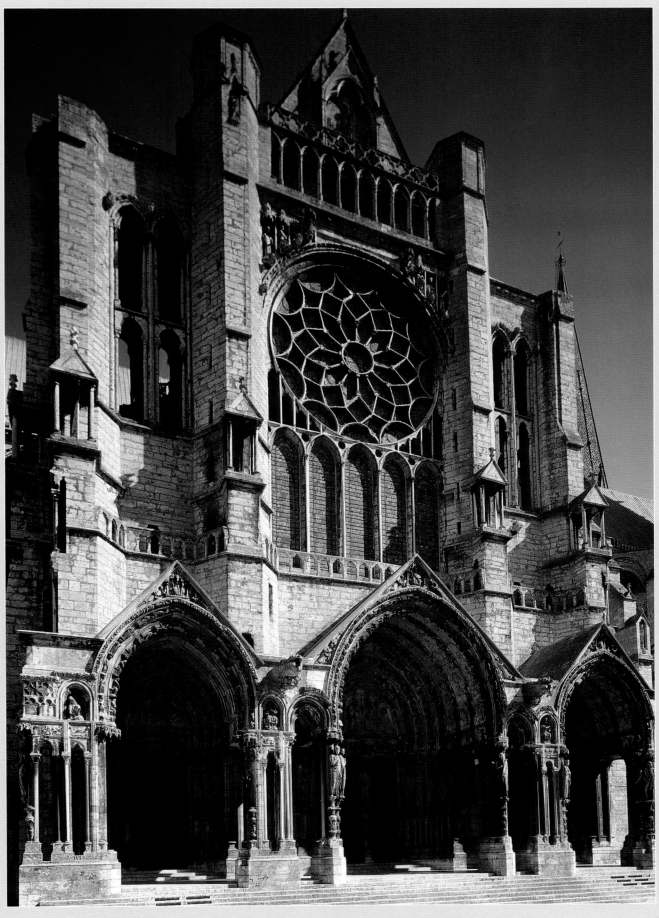

The spectacular cathedral at Chartres is a fine example of the detailed and intricate work masons undertook in their lifetimes

lifetime of their children. This was the age when the average life expectancy, even in a 'civilized' country like France, was less than forty years. The original cathedral in Chartres, one of the jewels in France's treasury of cathedrals, was begun in the eleventh century by Bishop Fulbert and was not finished until the second half of the following century. When it was destroyed by fire, work on the new one, which was built on the foundations of the old, started in 1194. It was over thirty years before it was ready to be consecrated, in an unfinished state.

Given the camaraderie (and rivalries) that must have existed between the builders, it is hardly surprising that the communities of masons were slowly transformed into professional brotherhoods. As we have seen, the Statutes of Ratisbon (and the subsequent Orders of Strasbourg) covered in some detail the rules covering the admission of apprentices, companions and masters. (In the same way, the rules of the various lodges of modern Freemasonry cover who can and cannot be admitted and the stages they must go through before being accepted into full membership of the lodge).

After serving as an apprentice for the required period, the young mason could be admitted to the lodge as a companion to finish his training. Or he could leave the lodge and travel to look for work at another construction site and seek admission in another lodge, to work for another Master.

Below the rank of Master was the man who transmitted the Master's advice, translating and explaining the often complex plans that the Master had drawn up. This lodge official was called, in Germany, the *parlier* from the French *parler*, which means 'to speak'.

The lodge members used signs of recognition, a tradition that is echoed in Freemasonry. But whereas some modern commentators see in these signs something esoteric and secret (adjectives that may well justifiably be applied to them as the years passed), they were an indication of one's membership of a body of equals who recognized one another as experts in a particular profession. These signs often found permanent expression in mason's marks, which were incised into stones to indicate who had put them in place, where they came from, or another piece of information that the men working on site liked or needed to know. The following describes some of the marks that were used.

The pieceworker's mark

As he was paid by the piece, the pieceworker was required to put his personal mark on each stone that he worked on to enable the Master to verify that the work had been completed to a satisfactory standard. Only then could the pieceworker be paid. The pieceworker's mark was usually very simple and geometric in style.

The positioning mark

This usually consisted of small engraved squares, crosses or arrows, indicating the direction in which the stones were to be placed. They were usually incised on the inside and hard to see once the stone was in place.

The mark of provenance

Usually incised on a side that was to be incorporated into the stonework of the building, these marks indicated where the stone had been quarried. When they were delivered to the building site, unskilled labourers would arrange them according to where they had come from so that the quantity from each quarry could be counted and the quarry paid the correct amount.

The Master's mark

Stonecutters and sculptors were given this mark by their peers, and it was used by them to 'sign' the most important pieces in the project. Once awarded, it was unique to that mason and was non-transferrable. Many of these marks, especially in Germany, incorporate the figure '4' in their design, not just as a mark of tribute to the Four Crowned Martyrs, but also to the fact that there were four major lodges of the Holy Roman Empire – Strasbourg, Cologne, Vienna and Rome.

The sign of Honour

The mark of a companion stonecutter, the sign of Honour was transformed into a unique crest which became the bearer's coat of arms and as such was incised on the stones for which he was responsible.

Working on any church building project was considered a privilege in those pious times. Being employed on a cathedral site was a great honour, no matter how humble the task. There is a tale, apocryphal perhaps but none the less charming for being so, of a very new apprentice who was working on the building of Strasbourg Cathedral under the ultimate tutelage of Jost Dotzinger, who presided over the gathering of stonecutters that formulated the Statutes of Ratisbon. While he was engaged in sweeping debris and rubble from a corner of the site, the young man was asked by a senior lodge member what he was about. 'Sir,' he replied, 'I am helping Master Dotzinger to build Strasbourg Cathedral.'

THE MASONS OF THE BRITISH ISLES

The rules and regulations of the British Masons were embodied in what is known as the Old Charges, the oldest copy of which is the *Regius Manuscript*, which is just one of the many priceless documents held by the British Museum and which is thought to date back to AD1390 (hence the archaic spellings in the quotes that follow).

The manuscript deals with the number of unemployed and the necessity of finding work 'that they myght gete here lyvynge thereby'. Whoever wrote the document seems to have consulted the works of Euclid, the Greek mathematician (300BC) who is hailed by many (and cursed by generations of schoolchildren) as 'the father of geometry'. This ancient scholar apparently recommended what the *Regius Manuscript* describes as the 'onest craft of good masonry' as found 'yn Egypte lande'. 'Mony eryes afterwards' we read the 'Craft com ynto England yn tyme of good king Adelstonus day'.

A ROYAL CHARTER

That was when Edwin, son of King Adelstonus or Athelstane (c. AD895–9), is believed to have presided over a meeting of the masons working on building the churches that would, much later, form part of the great York Minster. Athelstane is credited by many with establishing the York Rite Masonry and granting it a royal charter. Each year thereafter the masons held a general assembly which is credited with being the catalyst for the building of many building projects – castles, fortresses and abbeys – in which the masons' skills were put to extensive use.

It was at the meeting in York that the Charges were agreed.

The Charges, as well as referring to trade regulations, are an incentive to those who abide by them to discharge their obligations faithfully and fairly. Each member or brother was instructed:

> *He must love wel God, and holy Church algate*
> *and his mayster also, that he ys with.*

The document goes on:

> *The thrydde poynt must be severle*
> *With the prentis knowe hyt wele*
> *Hys mayster cownsel he kepe and close,*
> *And hys felows by hys goode purpose;*
> *The prevetyse of the chamber tell he no mon,*
> *Ny yn the logge whatsover they done,*
> *Whatsever thou heryst, or syste hem do,*
> *Telly hyt no mon, whersever thou go.*

And later it refers back to Euclid, who, in the language of medieval times:

The Charges

The preamble states that what follows is the worthy and godly oath of the masons and that every man that is a mason must take heed of this charge.

The first charge is that you shall be true unto God and the Holy Church, and that you use no heresy or error by your understanding or by teaching of indiscreet men.

~

Also you shall be true liegemen to the King without treason or falsehood and that you know no treason but that you amend it if you may or else warn the King or his Council thereof. Also you shall be true to one another, that is to say to every member and fellow of The Craft of masonry that be masons allowed and that you do to them as they would do to you.

~

And also that every mason keep counsel of lodge and chamber and all other counsel that ought to be kept by the way of masonry.

~

Also that no member be thief in Company so far forth that you shall know.

~

And also that you shall be true unto the lord and master that you serve and truly to see for his profit and advantage.

~

Also you do no villainy in that house whereby The Craft may be slandered.

These be the Charges in General which every mason should hold, both masters and fellows.

Now follow other Charges in particular for masters and fellows.

First that no master take upon him any lord's work nor other work but that he know himself unable to perform the same so that The Craft have no disworship but that the lord may be served truly.

~

Also that no master take any work that he take it reasonably so that the lord may be truly served with his own goods and that the master live honestly and truly pay his fellows their pay as the manner of The Craft does require.

~

Also that no master or fellow supplant other of their work (that is to say) if they have taken a work or stand master of a lord's work you shall not put him out unless he be unable to end the work.

~

Also that no master or fellow take any apprentice to be allowed his apprentice but for seven years and that the apprentice be able of birth and limbs as he ought to be.

Through hye grace of Crist yn Heven,
He commensed yn the syens seven.

Or, in more modern terms:

Through the grace of Christ in Heaven,
He began seven sciences.

The text goes on to name and explain these 'seven sciences' before detailing the Charges. Those listed in the *Cooke Manuscript* were probably taken from a version

Also that no master or fellow take allowance to be made mason without the assent of his fellows at the least five or six.

~

And also that is to be made freeborn of good kindred and no bondsman and that he have his right limbs, as a man ought to have.

~

Also that no master put a lord's work to task that was used to go to journey.

~

Also that every mason give pay to his fellows but as he may deserve so that he be not deceived by false workmen.

~

Also that no fellows slander another falsely behind his back to make him lose his good name or his worldly goods.

~

Also that no fellow withhold his lodge or without answer another ungodly without reasonable cause.

~

Also that every mason prefers his elder and put him to worship.

~

Also that no mason shall play cards hazards of any other unlawful game whereby they may be slandered.

~

Also that no mason commit ribaldry or lechery to make The Craft slandered and that no fellow go into the town where there is a lodge of masons without a fellow to bear him witness that he was in honest company.

~

Also that every master and fellow come to the assembly if he be within fifty miles and he have warning and to stand to the award of masters and fellows.

~

Also that every master and fellow if he have trespassed shall stand to the award of masters and fellows to make them accord and if they cannot to go to the Common law.

~

Also that no mason make moulds 'sware' or rule to any rough layers.

~

Also that no mason set layers within a lodge or without to have moulded stones with a mould of his own making.

~

Also that every mason shall receive and cherish strange masons when they came over the country and set them on work as the manner is (that is to say) if they have moulded stones in place he shall set him a fortnight on work at the least and give him his hire and there be no stones for him then to refresh him with some money to bring him to the next lodge, and also to every mason shall serve truly the works and truly make an end of the work be it task or Journey if he has pay as he ought to have.

These charges are here rehearsed and all other that belong to masonry you shall keep to the uttermost of your knowledge.

So help you God and by the contents of this Book.

earlier than the *Regius Manuscript.* The ones quoted above are from yet another medieval document, the *Beswicke-Royds Manuscript*, and are updated to twenty-first century spellings for ease of understanding.

Copies of all these and other manuscripts are available, and it is fascinating to think that in a time when only a handful of people could read and write, many stonemasons must have had these, to us, basic skills. Otherwise why did medieval scribes commit them to paper if none among the group at which they were aimed had the ability to read them?

The words may read oddly, but the spirit of the message they carry is one that is at the heart of modern Freemasonry.

William the Conqueror's victory at the Battle of Hastings in 1066 ushered in an era of church building which saw upwards of five thousand places of worship being built

AFTER THE NORMAN CONQUEST

Until the fourteenth century, there is scant evidence that the British masons were in any way organized or that there was much communication between the masons in one part of the land and those in another. But each new style of building spread across the country within a few years of it being introduced. In the thirty years following the Norman Conquest of 1066, more than five thousand new churches were built, those in the north being similar in size, proportion and layout to those in the south, three or four hundred miles away. To those of us who live in today's world of instant and instantaneous communication, that is no distance at all, but it was a different story a thousand years ago. The Norman style is obviously different from the churches that date from the years immediately before the Conquest, which is something that suggests a kind of central ecclesiastic planning authority. With no evidence of any such body, the uniformity of the change in church architecture was probably down to the masons travelling from site to site and taking the new ideas with them.

Operative masons (men who worked on church and other buildings) as opposed to elective masons (non-builders who were, much later, accepted into the lodges) were a mobile band of men travelling from place to place in search of work. From

Winchester in the south of England to Durham in the north, generations of craftsmen were at work on the glorious buildings that are, perhaps, one of the great legacies of the medieval Roman Catholic Church to future generations of Englishmen.

As he travelled round the country, a mason would hope to be accepted into the community of craftsmen already employed at any place he stopped. It is only to be expected that he would have to prove his credentials. This was not so much to guarantee his skills, as these would be tested as soon as he was put to work, but more because he needed to satisfy his employer and his peers that he was *au fait* with and had pledged his fidelity to The Craft, its customs and its code of practice. One way to establish bona fides was by the use of a system of secret signs known only to members of the mason's craft. These secret signs are echoed in those of Freemasonry, which enable members of The Craft to identify themselves to others in the movement.

CRAFT GUILDS

It was not just the masons who jealousy guarded their secrets from others. Other craftsmen, too, joined together to form guilds to secure uniform high standards of technical skills throughout their trade, no matter where it was practised, and to lay down rules for the better governance of their members. These guilds also had their trade secrets, but whereas the masons journeyed around the country, the guild members tended to stay put, following their careers in the same place their entire life.

Guild members knew one another. They made regular contributions to the common purse to ensure that sick members who were unable to work would not go hungry, to pay the funeral expenses of dead members whose families were unable to pay for a decent burial, and for a variety of other purposes. Guild members worshipped at the church where they maintained an altar dedicated to their patron saint, on whose festival day attendance was obligatory.

Because they moved from place to place across England and Scotland in search of work, individual masons were denied such permanence. They could be in York one year and Ripon the next if they were working for themselves. If they were employed by the monarch, they had to go wherever they were sent, perhaps to a new palace that was being built or to one which was being renovated.

Later in their history, in late Tudor and Stuart times, some masons formed themselves into guilds in conjunction with other building tradesmen, but generally their organization tended to be regional in character. That said, much of what we know of the way the guilds worked was incorporated into the Old Charges (see pp. 32-33).

The suggestion has been made that some modern Freemason ceremonies have their roots in the annual productions of miracle plays with which the guilds were widely associated. But in none of the four cycles of mystery plays still performed, or in any of

A medieval mystery play is performed in a cathedral precinct. The plays were frequently performed by members of craft guilds and drew their stories from ancient history

the other pageants of ceremonial events with which the masons were involved, is there anything to connect them with the masons. At least, almost nothing, for it is thought that in the early years there was a ritual based on the building of the Ark, something that features in the mystery and miracle plays.

THE BRITISH LODGES

As in continental Europe, the lodge was originally the place where the masons worked. The earliest reference to them eating and sleeping in the lodges in England dates from 1277 in the accounts concerning the building of a long-gone abbey, Vale Royal. Apparently *logias* and *mansiones* were built for the workers so that they could live and work more or less on site and save them from having to travel to work from the nearest village, which was usually some distance away.

We do not know when the word 'lodge' came to be used to describe the community rather than the building. But in the minutes of Scotland's Aitchison Lodge that date from 1598, and from statutes of the same and the following year, reference is made to the Edinburgh, Kilwinning and Stirling Lodges.

The names used for each level in the strict hierarchy that existed within the medieval lodges will be familiar to modern Freemasons.

GRADES

Apprentices

All the guilds taught their crafts to apprentices, who in turn passed them on to the next generation. In Britain, the earliest known regulation concerning their welfare dates back to around 1320, a century or so before apprenticeships began to be insisted upon by craft guilds and became widespread.

There are few references to masons' apprentices, probably because what we know about the early days of stonemasonry comes from the accounts of large-scale building projects, and apprentices were too low down the hierarchy to merit much mention.

The term 'entered apprentice' first features in English in 1723, in the *Book of Constitutions*, more than 120 years after it is known that it was a feature of Scottish masonry. It was standard practice for an apprentice who had completed his seven-year indenture to be entered into the lodge as an entered apprentice. Unlike their indentured brothers they were allowed to do some work on their own initiative, but they were not free to employ subordinates.

Fellows

The period of entered apprenticeship varied from lodge to lodge, but seven years seems to have been the norm. So, a Scottish lad just into his teens who was apprenticed to a mason, could be in his mid-twenties – having served a seven-year apprenticeship and another seven years as an entered apprentice – before being admitted as a Fellow of Craft. He was now entitled to take on contracts that involved employing others. By the end of the sixteenth century, the grades Entered Apprentice and Fellow of Craft had lost their practical significance.

The term is also first mentioned in England in the *Book of Constitutions*, but the word 'Fellow' is known to have been used in this context by the end of the fourteenth century, although it seems not to have bestowed any grade superiority on those to whom the word was applied. Rather it was used to indicate a member of a fraternity. A century later, it seems to have acquired the same meaning as it had in Scotland, indicating a man who was superior to ordinary masons and was entitled to employ them.

Warden

The office from which the Masonic term is derived started to appear around the end of the fourteenth century. In York, in 1408, the Warden and other senior masons

took an oath of loyalty not just to the Master but to the regulations as well. In London at the end of the fifteenth century, there are several instances of the Warden being responsible for the lodge's financial affairs.

Work began on London's Westminster Hall during the reign of William II (1097-99) and continued for many years

The Master Mason

Up to the beginning of the eighteenth century, the term Master Mason was applied only to the mason who was in charge of a building project. The office is first recorded as being used in reference to John of Gloucester, who was in charge of constructing London's glorious Westminster Hall in the mid-thirteenth century. The hall was the scene of many famous trials, including that of King Charles I in 1649, and more recently it was where US President Reagan addressed the assembled Houses of Parliament. Today, more than 750 years after work commenced on the building, it stands as an awe-inspiring tribute to Master Mason Gloucester and the other masons who worked on it.

North of the border, it was only towards the end of the seventeenth century that the term 'Master Mason' was used. Until then the 'master mason' was called Deacon or Warden and sometimes Preses. By the time the term was in common usage in

Scottish lodges, members were being elected to lodge membership, and it is not clear whether 'Master Masons' presided over operative lodges.

'Free' masons

The first known use of the term 'free mason' dates from 1376, when it seems to have been used to differentiate between two classes of mason. The lower was the vassal mason, who owed allegiance to the master mason in much the same way that an agricultural serf owed his to the lord of the manor on which he lived. The superior of the two appears to have been a 'better' class of operative mason, but the distinction between them has been clouded by the mists of history, and, indeed, there may not have been any practical difference between the two.

By the seventeenth century, the term 'freemason' was beginning to be applied to non-operative masons, members of a lodge who had no association with the craft of stoneworking.

Historians are divided as to what the term 'freemason' means. Some think it was used to imply that whoever was so called was free from the restrictive practices and regulations that were common in Britain. He may have been free from the widespread tolls and taxes. Or it could have been that he was free to practise his craft anywhere he could find work.

Another theory is that the 'free' mason was permitted to work wherever his skills were needed, unlike senior members of other guilds, who were granted the freedom of the city or borough in order to carry on their businesses within the city borders. The mason's craft, however, was one that required him to work wherever there was a large-scale building project.

Another school of thought has it that 'freemasons' were skilled craftsmen who cut and shaped superior quality stone known as freestone that was found in only a few quarries in an area that stretched from Dorset in the south of England more than 300 kilometres to the northeast. Some freestone was also imported from sites in Normandy in northern France. Cutting fine quality stone required more skill than stone of lesser quality, or 'rough stone'as it was known, which could not be properly squared.

The most likely explanation is that the 'free' in 'freemasonry' meant different things at different times in history.

The Layer

The term 'layer' (also called 'setter') is one that is often found in the accounts of early building projects. Their chief tool was one that in the layman's eyes is often associated with Freemasonry: the trowel.

Layers were a separate class of workmen who were employed to build up the stones that the masons had prepared. Less skilled than the men at the top of the lodge, the Layers nonetheless were conscious of their position and were often at odds with the masons. Evidence exists that because the builders' craft was a peripatetic one, when masons finished one job and went in search of another, if there was no suitable mason's position available, they would accept work as a Layer. Similarly, if no mason was available, a setter may have been promoted to the mason's role.

There is evidence that demarcation disputes between masons and Layers were not unknown in the fourteenth century in London,. In fact, relations between the two classes seem to have degenerated to such an extent that they had to be regulated. In 1360 it was enacted that every mason 'shall be compelled by his master whom he serveth to do every work pertaining to do, or of free stone or of rough stone'.

The Cowan

In 1598 the Scottish Schaw Statutes referred to a class of working mason who, despite having served a proper apprenticeship, had not been admitted into a lodge (and was therefore not a member of what by then was known as 'the Fraternity'). Although they were trained and capable of worthwhile work, the cowan was

shunned by his fellows. In the words of the statute, 'Item, that no master or fellow craft receive a cowan to work in his society, or company, nor send any of his servants to work with cowans under pain of twenty pounds so oft as any person offends in this respect.'

Just over a hundred years later, in 1707, the minutes of the Mother Kilwinning Lodge read: 'No Meason [sic] shall employ no cowan which is to say without the word to work.' The common omission of the last two words has led to a cowan being defined as 'a mason without the word'.

There is no record of the cowan in English masonry until 1738, when the term was recorded by James Anderson in his second *Book of Constitutions*.

A 14th century representation of the plague. The Black Death caused an acute labour shortage throughout Europe

THE ASSEMBLY

A governing body, or 'assembly' of all the lodges in England, is mentioned in the Old Charges as meeting periodically and having legislative powers over the lodges' activities. Every Master Mason was expected to attend and to report back to his lodge. The Assembly, if it ever did exist for there is no contemporary evidence of it, may have met annually or every third year.

Those who believe that the Assembly did meet cite as evidence two statutes, the first of 1360 and the second of 1425, which banned congregations of masons. But as with much that is concerned with Freemason history, opinion is divided. Sceptics say that the statutes were not concerned with any assemblies of masons, but rather they were to do with banning illegal organizations that had been established to fight for higher wages and better working conditions.

*King's College, Cambridge was founded by Henry VI in 1445, although work was not completed until 1515.
Its magnificent ceiling is a fine example of the intricacies of the masons' skills*

EDWARD III-ELIZABETH I

The statutes were not the first pieces of legislation concerning masons that had been put on the books. The Statute of Labourers of 1350 had prescribed the money that masons could earn. The statute had been deemed necessary because the Black Death was causing an acute labour shortage. The plague had swept in from Asia and across Europe, reaching England in 1348. Within 12 months or so as much as an eighth of the population had been killed. The simple law of supply and demand (there was a demand for the masons' skills and a decreased supply of masons to fulfil it) was causing their wages to rise to unprecedented levels. One of the principal employers was the king, Edward III, and he decided to do something about it: 'Item, that carpenters, masons and tilers and other workmen of houses shall not take their work, but in such manner as they were wont: that is to say . . . a master freestone mason 3d, and other masons 3d . . . and their servants 1d.' Ten years later, it was declared in another statute: 'All alliances and convenes of masons and carpenters, and congregations, chapters ordinances and other oaths betwixt them . . . shall be henceforth void and wholly annulled.'

By Elizabeth I's reign the distinction between masons involved in construction work and Freemasons was lost

In 1425 an act was passed that ordained that 'Congregations and Confederacies' made by the masons in 'their general chapters assembled . . . be openly violated and broken. Our said Lord hath ordained and established that . . . Masons that come into such Congregations and Confederacies be punished by imprisonment of their bodies and make fine and ransom at the king's will.'

In his *Book of Constitutions*, James Anderson has it that the king in question, Henry VI, later became a Freemason himself. If true, he may have been well suited to the honour. He was said to be kind and generous, a simple man who was regarded as being incapable of craftiness or any kind of deceit.

Operative masons were hard at work during his reign, as Henry was an enthusiastic builder. Among the works for which he was responsible is King's College in Cambridge. Famous for its annual carol service, the building is also noted for the magnificent fan vaulting in the ceiling.

By Elizabeth I's reign, in England, it seems that the 'mason' of 'freemason' had lost much of its operative meaning. In 1563 an act was passed that referred to 'roughe masons'. Until then, the term 'mason' or 'freemason' had been used, so it seems that there was now an accepted distinction between masons who worked on construction works and freemasons who had little to do with the builder's craft.

But the legacy of the masons lives on. We can see it for ourselves in the churches and cathedrals that were built during the Middle Ages – built for the glory of God.

ON SINE SOLE IRIS

EMERGENCE

*Freemasonry may, indeed, been formally established in London in 1717,
but it is much older than the 400 or so years that have elapsed since the
members of four London lodges made their way to St Paul's to sup
and do their business. As we have seen, Freemasonry's roots may
extend far beyond London: they stretch all over Europe and perhaps into
the Middle East . . .*

That events of 1717 were recorded by James Anderson, often regarded as 'the Father of Masonic History'. In the first *Book of Constitutions* Anderson wrote that the newly elected Grand Master was the latest in a long line of men who had held the post. He claimed that, having led the Israelites from Egypt, Moses often marshalled his people 'into a regular and general lodge while in the wilderness'. He claimed that Nebuchadrezzar had been the Grand Master Mason.

THE EARLY BRITISH FREEMASONRY

In the second edition of the work, published in 1738 and dedicated to the Prince of Wales, 'Master Mason and Master of a Lodge,' Anderson writes that Cyrus, ruler of Persia (*c*. 500BC) constituted Jerubabbell 'Provincial Grand Master in Judea.' He goes on to write that Charles Martel, who defeated the Moors at Poitiers in AD732, was 'The Right Worshipful Grand Master of France', and that Edward I (1239–1307), being 'heavily engaged in wars, left the craft to the care of several successive grand masters'.

Few people would deny that much of what Anderson wrote can fairly be described as complete nonsense, but there is no doubt that the members of the four lodges who met at the Goose and Gridiron early in 1717 were the heirs of a long and honourable tradition.

The Goose and Gridiron Lodge was itself founded in 1691, in the same year that Sir Christopher Wren is thought to have been adopted as a 'brother' at a Masonic convention held in St Paul's Church.

The records of Edinburgh Mary's Chapel lodge – assumed to be the oldest records in the world – date back almost a century before that, to 1599. And the word 'Freemason' itself first appeared in statute, and in an act passed during Henry VII's reign (1485–1509).

That mention was 20 years or so after the London Company of Freemasons was granted a coat of arms in 1473. It included in its design 'a feld of Sablys, a chevron silver-grailed three Castellis of the same garnyshed wt. Dores and wyndiws of the field in the Cehevron or Cumpas of Black of Blak'. This is the origin for all later armorial bearings having a chevron and castles that were subsequently assumed by other Masonic organizations.

Just over a century later, in 1583, James VI, Mary Queen of Scots' son, who in 1603 ascended the joint thrones of England and Scotland as James I, appointed William Schaw as his Master of Works and Warden General. In 1598, Schaw issued the first of the famous statutes, which set out the duties that lodge members owed to their lodges. It also laid down penalties that members had to pay if they were responsible for unsatisfactory work or if they worked with unqualified masons.

A year later, Schaw drew up a second statute in which we find the first reference

*Nebuchadrezzar, king of Babylon is considered by some to be one of a line of Grand Master Masons
that stretches back into distant history*

The Banqueting Hall in London's Whitehall was designed by Inigo Jones who is believed to have been entered into one of the capital's lodges

to esoteric knowledge within the 'Craft of stone masonry'. In other words, men with no experience of or connection with practical masonry were being admitted to lodges.

The Second Statute also reveals that the Mother Lodge of Scotland, Lodge Kilwinning No. 0 was in existence at the time. When it was actually founded we don't know. Nor do we know if it was founded before, after or at the same time as Edinburgh's Mary Chapel Lodge. The dispute as to which is the older (Stirling and Scone also have their claimants) is unlikely to be settled one way or the other, but, interestingly, both sides can find backing for their claim in Schaw's Second Statute.

Kilwinning may be a small town in the west of Scotland, but it plays a significant part in Masonic history. A monastery was founded there in 1140, and it is more than likely that a lodge was formed around the same time. According to those who back Kilwinning's claim, Robert the Bruce instituted the Royal Order of Herodem after the Battle of Bannockburn in 1314 and reserved for himself and his successors the title of Grand Master of the Royal Grand Lodge of Herodem at Kilwinning.

Schaw's regulations also required all lodges to keep records, to meet at specific times and to test members on their knowledge of the 'Art of Masonry'.

The first record of the initiation of an accepted mason (one with no connection with the actual craft of masonry) is that of James Boswell, Laird of Auchenleck, an ancestor of Dr Johnson's famous biographer, who was initiated in Edinburgh in 1600.

It seems that Freemasonry was also flourishing in England by this time, and a few years after James VI ascended the English throne he declared himself Freemasonry's protector. Among the men thought to have been accepted into a Masonic lodge during James' reign was Inigo Jones, the celebrated architect. Jones was the first English architect to adapt Italian ideas, particularly those of Palladio (from whom we get the word 'Palladium') to English requirements.

In 1615 he became surveyor-general of royal buildings, and a year later he began work on the beautiful Queen's House at Greenwich. He was also responsible for the Banqueting House in London's Whitehall, and the celebrated Double Cube Room at Wilton House, a few miles west of Salisbury in Wiltshire.

Today's Freemasons who visit Freemason's Hall in London's Great Queen Street can see something of Jones's work a short walk away in Covent Garden where the recently restored Piazza was built to Jones's plans.

ACCEPTED MASONS

By the middle of the century, it was becoming increasingly common for eminent men to be initiated into lodges as honorary members or accepted masons. It was at this time, in 1646, that Elias Ashmole was initiated, on 16 October at Warrington in Lancashire. He is probably the first non-operative mason to have been accepted into an English lodge, or 'made', although there is some evidence that an English colonel was initiated into an operative lodge five or six years earlier.

Ashmole had qualified as a lawyer eight years earlier and combined an active political role, supporting the Royalist cause against Cromwell's Parliamentarians, with studying mathematics, physics, astrology and alchemy. A lifelong collector of antiquities and rarities, he presented his hoard – much of which had been bequeathed to him by his old friend and fellow antiquarian John Tradescant – to his old university, Oxford, where he had studied at Brasenose. The collection was eventually housed in a specially built museum, the Ashmolean, in that city. His life encapsulates several of Freemasonry's Five Virtues – Tolerance, Achievement, Charity, Integrity and Fidelity.

Elias Ashmole's Royalist principles and his father-in-law's Parliamentarian views were no bar to both being members of the same lodge. The men were said to be the first non-operative or speculative masons to be accepted into a lodge

45

The meeting of the Warrington Lodge at which Ashmole was accepted appears to have been called specifically for that purpose. He recorded the event in his diary and in the same volume mentions a visit to a lodge in London in 1682, by which time it appears that non-operative masons had become more and more common.

The question as to why this happened at this time has intrigued many historians. One of them, Colin Dyer, has pointed out that Ashmole, a die-hard royalist, was initiated during the English Civil War. England was in turmoil. Roman Catholics were being viewed with increasing hatred, devout members of the faith being forced to hear the Mass in secret. The Catholic priests risked life and limb to give Holy Communion to recusant families who refused to give up their faith. The political spectrum had narrowed to Royalist on one side and Parliamentarian on the other, with no space in between for any other opinion.

Communities were split and families were divided. But there were men who passionately believed in freedom of speech, men who recognized the need for a forum where people of different beliefs and political points of view could meet and discuss their opinions harmoniously. Dyer argues that these men came together to form a 'fraternal order' firmly rooted in the belief in God and the freedom of speech.

Among these men, Dyer writes, were Elias Ashmole, who was held prisoner by the Parliamentarians for his views, and his father-in-law, Henry Mainwairing, a colonel in the Parliamentarian army. They held widely differing views, but each respected the other and both were initiated into the same lodge at the same time.

Dyer believes that Ashmole and his like-minded brethren saw in the building of King Solomon's Temple a perfect allegory for their belief that a better world could be built on the firm foundations of Brotherly Love and Truth. They adopted the masons' tools as their symbols and adapted the old Masonic lodges to their purpose, and Dyer believes that this is the true origin of today's Freemasonry.

Even when the Civil War was over, and even after Oliver Cromwell died and Charles II was restored to the throne in 1660, religious and political intolerance continued. The Stuarts' rule, with their belief in their 'Divine Right' to rule came to an end in 1688, when the openly Roman Catholic James II (his brother, Charles II, had been baptized into the faith on his deathbed) fled the country. The throne passed to the joint rule of James' daughter Mary II and her Dutch husband William III, and with them a new era of tolerance was eventually ushered in. Even so, it was not until the failure of the Jacobite Revolution of 1715, which aimed to restore James II's son to the throne, that open political debate and freedom of conscience were, if not guaranteed, at least not put down.

Colin Dyer believes that it was then that the Freemasons could openly proclaim themselves and that the time was right for the founding of the Grand Lodge.

Thirty-odd years before that, by 1686, Freemasonry *per se* was widespread enough to warrant mention in Robert Plant's *The Natural History of Shropshire*. It is claimed that by the following decade there were as many as seven lodges operating in London and another in York. Several more had been established by the turn of the century, including one in Scarborough.

As the years passed, more and more men with no connection with masonry *per se* – 'speculative' or 'accepted masons' – were initiated into lodges which had been established centuries before by men who had spent years, decades perhaps, learning the craft of masonry.

What was it that attracted these men into the lodges?

Was it the fellowship of like minds?

Was it for convivial evenings spent among men from the same educated background?

Was it, as Colin Dyer, suggests, the recognition of a need for a forum where men who believed passionately in freedom of speech and worship could discuss their views without fear of persecution.

Or was it, as W. Kirk McNulty suggests in his book *Freemasonry: A Journey Through Ritual and Symbol*, a shared interest in the mystical and mysterious traditions of the Kabbalists?

McNulty writes of Freemasonry in the second half of the seventeenth century:

'On the one hand there is a prominent body of influential and educated men who are known to be interested in the Hermetic/Kabbalastic tradition. And during the turbulent middle years of the century [seventeenth] have found it necessary to be more guarded in the pursuit of their interests. On the other hand there is an operative Builders Guild in decline, which by 1665 is known to have an increased membership of gentlemen whose interests are in the mystical tradition believed to be preserved at the core of the guild.'

Perhaps it was a combination of all these factors – conviviality, fellowship and mystery, the last one giving Freemasonry the reputation of being a 'secret society' whose use of symbols and ritual – that did much to encourage that reputation. And being a member of a secret society has a certain thrill which many find attractive.

THE GRAND LODGE

Whichever the reason, by 1717, Freemasonry had become sufficiently popular among men of a certain standing, for the members of London's four 'Old Lodges' to meet together and found the Premier Grand Lodge at the much aforementioned Goose and Gridiron ale house, in London on 24 June of that year.

After electing Anthony Sayer, the oldest Master Mason, 'and then a Master of a Lodge' as their Grand Master, the members agreed to meet together once a year thereafter to hold a 'Grand Feast'. Sayer appointed Grand Wardens and 'commanded the Master and Wardens of Lodges to meet the Grand Officers' four times a year 'in Communication'.

Whether or not these meetings ever took place is not recorded; certainly there is no evidence that they ever did. But we do know that members of the four London lodges did meet every year to enjoy the prescribed Grand Feast.

There is also no record of the Grand Lodge in London in its very early years having any desire or intention of seeking to control the activities of the lodges in other parts of England. It was, essentially, a London club. But Anthony Sayer's successors in the post of Grand Master had other ideas.

Sayer's immediate successors, George Payne and Theophilus Desaguliers, stamped their own ideas on Freemasonry. In 1720, Payne codified the regulations of the Grand Lodge. Three years later it was decided to elect a Grand Secretary, and on his appointment the practice of taking minutes of each meeting was established.

The first man appointed to the post was William Cowper of the Horn Lodge, his appointment being noted in The First Minute Book of the Grand Lodge of England, which is the first official record of speculative Freemasonry, and is dated 24 June 1723.

That same year, James Anderson, a clergyman like Desaguliers, published the first official *Constitution of the Freemasons*. The constitution is a marriage of The Old Charges as laid down in the Regus and other medieval manuscripts and Anderson's imaginative retelling of the mystical origins of The Craft.

Desaguliers was the son of French Huguenot refugees. As well as being a clergyman, he was a respected scientist (he invented the planetarium) and was especially interested in what he called 'The Hidden Mysteries of Nature and Science'. He counted among his friends Sir Isaac Newton and many members of the influential and prestigious Royal Society. Many of the Society's Fellows, influenced by Desaguliers'

The sign of the Goose and Gridiron, the inn in St Paul's churchyard that was the meeting place of London's four 'Old Lodges' that led to the foundation of the England's Grand Lodge

example, became Freemasons themselves, and twelve of his successors as Grand Master were also Fellows of the Society. Others were elected Grand Officers, one of whom, Martin Folkes, for twelve years the Society's president, introduced Alexander Pope and Jonathan Swift into The Craft.

Pope and Swift, satirists as they were, were obviously attracted by Freemasonry's aims and ideals. So was the artist, William Hogarth, who used pen and ink as the medium of his satirical eye. The fact that he was a Mason and a Grand Steward of his lodge did not stop him lampooning The Craft in at least one of his works, *Night*, which shows a Freemason returning home from a lodge meeting very much

It was images such as this, of a nineteenth-century Masonic Grand Feast, that fixed the idea in the minds of many that Freemasonry was the exclusive domain of upper-class men who met to eat and drink too much

the worse for wear. It wasn't just men of letters and of the arts who were attracted to the aims and ideals of Freemasonry: British princes and royal dukes were early members of the Grand Lodge. Within three years of its founding, every Grand Master of the Grand Lodge was either of royal or noble blood, a tradition that lasted for many years.

Perhaps it was this that caused The Grand Lodge increasingly to be seen as a meeting place for men from London society's upper echelons, and any lingering influence that the old operative element had soon evaporated. The guilds of the men who had built the medieval cathedrals and royal palaces of England had

William Hogarth's satirical painting Night *shows a drunk freemason returning from a lodge meeting*

become, in the eyes of some members and many outsiders, a club for the heirs of the men who had commissioned their work.

Within a few years of its foundation, the influence of the Grand Lodge had grown, with more and more provincial lodges coming to accept its authority. Perhaps the members of these out-of-town lodges were influenced by the idea of being associated, however loosely, with the noblemen and gentlemen who attended the Grand Lodge. A few lodges, however, held on to their independence, notably in York, where a separate and independent tradition was established with its own Grand Lodge.

As the Industrial Revolution gained momentum, England's cities expanded and a new class of men appeared wealthy industrialists who were keen to be accepted into society as 'gentlemen'. And if making it known that they would not be unwilling to be accepted into a lodge with links via the Grand Lodge and therefore by association, albeit tenuous, with royalty and nobility, then so much the better. As a result, in many areas of England, Freemasonry spread its branches wider and flourished while in some rural areas with a declining population, some lodges lost so many members that they withered and perished.

Gone, long gone, were the days when masons met in lodges on or close to the sites where they worked. Still to come were the days when they were to meet in temples and halls richly adorned with the allegorical symbolism with which modern Freemasonry is associated in the minds of many. The Freemasons of the early eighteenth century met in inns and coffee houses, renting a room where they held their lodge meetings.

DRAWING THE LODGE

It was at these meetings that new members were admitted. (Details may have changed but by and large a lodge meeting progresses now much as it did in these early days.) Before the assembly, a large oblong table was set up in the middle of the room and the necessary tools and properties were removed from the lodge box where they were normally kept and put in place on it.

The members of the lodge and its appointed officers then assembled. The most important was (and is) the Master who administered the lodge and was responsible for conducting its ceremonies. He was (and is) assisted by two Wardens. Immediately below the Wardens are two Deacons whose job it still is to relay the wishes and instructions of the Master to the Wardens. The Deacons also conduct candidates for admissions and guide them through the rituals of the ceremony to come.

In the early days, before the introduction of the table cloths and Tracing Boards which are now used to display the emblems and symbols of each of the degrees, these symbols were drawn on the floor in chalk, a ritual known as 'drawing the lodge'.

Candidates for admission were (and still are) kept out of the lodge until the required time by a Guardian of the Lodge, known as the Outer Guard or Tyler. He is also responsible for keeping out any intruders and for preparing the candidate for admission.

When the lodge was in order and the candidate readied by the Tyler, he was then admitted through the door by the Junior Warden or the Steward. This function has now been taken over by a second Guard, the Inner Guard.

Once admitted into the room, the candidate was required to swear on the Bible an Obligation to maintain and preserve the mysteries of The Craft. That done, the

Coffee houses were meeting places for Freemasons in the eighteenth century. Other patrons' rowdy behaviour, such as the type seen here, would not be tolerated by Masonic lodges

entrant was then given the Mason Word and Sign and he was read the Charges, which laid out his duty to God, to his Master and to his fellow men. The history of The Craft, dating back to the building of Solomon's Temple was related as part of the Charges.

By the time the Grand Lodge was formed, a two-tier system of Entered Apprentice and Fellow Craft had been established. Within a few years of its establishment, a third degree, the Master Mason, had been introduced, by which time the ceremony had become more elaborate.

A physical penalty was introduced along with the Obligation, and after the appropriate Word and Sign had been communicated, the candidate was subject to a short catechism. This explained the details of the ceremony and the symbolism of the tools appropriate to the level to which the candidate was being admitted. A pictorial and symbolic representation of the principles applying to each degree would then be seen on the appropriate Tracing Board, which, in medieval times, was the board on which the architect or builder traced out the ground plan of the building to be constructed.

As the candidate goes through the ceremonies of the three Craft Degrees, from Apprentice to Fellow Craft to Master Mason, he is made aware of the need to maintain his faith in God or the Supreme Being. He is encouraged to hope that he will find salvation and to be aware that in his dealings with his fellow men he should be charitable in everything he does.

Next, the importance of understanding the hidden mysteries of Nature and Science (something that so fascinated Theophilus Desagulier) is stressed through the study of the seven liberal arts and sciences – Grammar, Rhetoric, Logic, Arithmetic, Geometry, Music and Astronomy.

Lastly, the need to maintain honour at all times, to accept death as inevitable and to face it with stoicism and fortitude, being certain of immortality, is instilled into the candidate.

A French cloth showing the symbols of the First (Apprentice) Degree. In the days before cloths were introduced, these symbols were drawn in chalk on the floor of the lodge

The principles by which Freemasons live their lives, their ideals and the qualities they should strive to achieve, are represented in today's Masonic temples and permanent lodges in decoration and ornamentation built into the fabric of the lodge. They were and are seen in the pictorial diagrams for Apprentice, Fellow Craft and Master Mason on the Tracing Boards and also in the working tools that the relevant operative masons used as part of their day-to-day lives. To the Freemason, these tools represent psychological capacities he must identify, learn to control and then use as part of his day-to-day life.

The tools of the First Degree or Apprentice Freemason are the gavel, the chisel and the measuring rule. The first represents passion, the second analysis and the third measurement, something that defines the relationship between the first two. These are the tools of action that suit the Apprentice to the physical world.

The tools of the Second Degree or Fellow Craft are the level, the plumb rule and the set square. These are the symbolic tools of individual morality, which the Fellow Craft must put to use within himself, to test his own actions against the standards of Justice (represented by the level) and Mercy (represented by the plumb rule). The set square fulfils the same function for the Fellow Craft as the measuring rule does for the Apprentice, defining as it does the relationship between the other two, in this case Justice and Mercy.

The Working Tools of the Third Degree are tools of design, that is, for planning and for laying out work, which relate to the spirit. They are the pencil, the skirret and the compasses.

Once the ceremony was complete, the Apprentice entered, the Apprentice made Fellow Craft, the Fellow Craft made Mas-

ter Mason, the chalk circle that had 'drawn' the lodge was erased by the candidate with a bucket and mop. Now any other lodge business was finalized and the members enjoyed the Festive Board, at which it was the Steward's responsibility to serve the wine.

Overseeing the ritual and ceremonial of the lodge was the responsibility of the Director of Ceremonies, who was once known as the Master of Ceremonies. Other offices included Treasurer and Secretary, whose titles define their duties.

An apprentice is entered into a lodge in the early eighteenth century. Scenes such as this would normally have taken place in semi-darkness

THE PROVINCIAL GRAND LODGES

As more and more men were initiated into more and more lodges, it became difficult for the Grand Lodge, situated as it was in London, to administer the new lodges effectively. Today, in the age of e-mails, faxes and telephones, communication between one part of the world and another is more or less instant, but in the eighteenth century, things were quite different. The speed of communication

between one part of the country and the next was dependent on the speed of the horses available to carry what was to be communicated! So it was difficult for the Grand Lodge to be in effective, day-to-day control of the increasing number of lodges being established in the provinces.

To get round this, Provincial Grand Lodges were established along existing county lines, the main purpose of these lesser lodges being to constitute new lodges in their areas. It was not until 1813, when a United Grand Lodge of England was founded, with one of George III's younger sons, Augustus Frederick, Duke of Sussex, as Grand Master, that the Provincial Lodges had any clearly defined function.

NORTH OF THE BORDER AND ACROSS THE IRISH SEA

As we have seen, the earliest operative lodge in Scotland, be it Kilwinning No 0 or one of the other candidates for the honour, seems to have been in existence since at least the fourteenth century. And as we have also seen, one James Boswell was introduced into the Mary Lodge in Edinburgh in 1600, apparently as a non-operative or speculative Mason.

Given that long history, it may seem surprising that a Scottish Grand Lodge was not formed until almost 20 years after the English Grand Lodge was first called to order. But in Scotland, although there was a long tradition of masonic lodges, they retained their operative character far longer than seems to have been the case south of the Border.

On 30 November 1736 (St Andrew's Day), however, four old Scottish lodges combined to form the Scottish Grand Lodge. The man elected to be the Grand Master Mason of Scotland was William St Clair, whose ancestors had built Rosslyn Chapel (see p. 20) and whose family had long regarded itself as the hereditary heads of the Masonic movement in Scotland.

Within a few years, dissension arose between Kilwinning and other lodges as to which had historical precedence over the others. In 1743 Edinburgh's Canongate Kilwinning Lodge asserted its independence of the Scottish Grand Lodge, and for the next 70 years chartered lodges both in Scotland and later in America.

Two years after Kilwinning left the Scottish Grand Lodge, James II's grandson, Charles Edward Stuart, 'Bonnie Prince Charlie', landed with a handful of men on the west coast of Scotland to rally men to the Jacobite cause and restore the Stuart succession to the British throne.

Officially, the Grand Lodge took no definite stance, but, being men of strong political opinion, some individual Freemasons argued for the Protestant Hanoverians who had acceded to the British throne in 1714 on the death of Queen Anne, and others for the Catholic Stuarts.

The Kilwinning lodges were much more definite in their views. Almost to a man they supported the Jacobite cause and although there is no direct evidence, it is more than likely that they lent active support to the Young Pretender and his cause, something that fuelled the antagonism that existed between the Grand Lodge and the dissenting Kilwinning Lodges. It was only after the rebellion was crushed in 1746 at the Battle of Culloden and its brutal aftermath that 'friendly' relations between the two were restored, both sides viewing the English as a common enemy.

Meanwhile, across the Irish Sea, on 26 June 1725, the Earl of Rosse was elected Grand Master of the Grand Lodge in Dublin. The minutes of the meeting has Rosse as the 'New' Grand Master, which would seem to suggest that others had held the honour before him. But the only mention of Freemasonry in Ireland prior to 1725 is one mention in a literary work of there being a speculative lodge in Dublin, 37 years earlier.

Freemasonry soon spread throughout the country, some lodges heeding the directives that the Dublin Grand Lodge issued, others ignoring them and going their own way. A year after the Grand Lodge was established, a rival independent Grand Lodge of Munster was founded in Cork. It survived until 1733 when it seems to have submitted to Dublin's authority, as the rest of the Irish lodges eventually did, until the early nineteenth century when a Grand Lodge was founded in Ulster

which challenged the Dublin Grand Lodge's supremacy, albeit briefly. The differences between the two were soon settled and since then Dublin's Grand Lodge of Ireland has been Freemasonry's sole authority in Ireland.

It is to The Craft's eternal credit that in Ireland, where the divide between Catholic and Protestant has been a source of constant trouble for so many years, the members of both faiths were willing to lay aside their religious differences and enter Freemasonry's lodges together throughout the land. It was only when Freemasonry was accused of playing a part in the French Revolution that many Catholics followed the example of the Irish patriot Daniel O'Connell and resigned from their lodges. Many historians trace back the widening rift between Catholic and Protestant that blighted Irish history for much of the nineteenth and most of the twentieth centuries to this exodus of Catholics from The Craft.

In the predominantly Protestant north, which remained part of the United Kingdom after the Republic of Ireland was created in 1921, there is confusion in the minds of some that Freemasonry became the domain of Orangemen, the name deriving from William of Orange, who became William III on the 'abdication' of

Augustus Frederick, Duke of Sussex, who was elected Grand Master of the United Grand Lodge in 1813

During the 1745 Jacobite Rebellion, Scottish Freemasons were divided in their support for Bonnie Prince Charlie, although members of Kilwinning Lodge were unanimous in their backing for him and lent active support to his cause

James II. The annual marches of the Orange lodges every July that commemorate the anniversary of the Battle of the Boyne, in which William's army defeated Catholic supporters of James, became in the late twentieth century 'troubles' the focus of Catholic–Protestant rivalry. Orange lodges operate separately from regular Freemasonry, which abhors religious intolerance.

THE 'ANTIENTS'

In every club, in every movement, there are those who favour changes and those who oppose them. Freemasonry was to be no exception. Within a decade of the founding of the Grand Lodge in London, changes began to be introduced in some of the rituals and customs that many members held dear. Individually, these changes amounted to very little. Collectively, many Freemasons saw them as an unwarranted and unwanted intrusion into the practices they regarded.

At around the same time that discontent was beginning to be rear its head in some quarters, a group of Irishmen who had been members of lodges in 'the old country' were refused admission to London lodges. The fact that they were artisans and members of the capital's lodges tended to be gentlemen was part of the reason. More important was the fact that the Irish rituals that they practised did not conform to the English ones.

In 1751, the discontented English Masons decided to join their Irish brothers and formed six new lodges. In addition they set up a Grand Committee, which by 1753 had become a Grand Lodge that was running independently of the original one. Claiming to have restored all the original customs, rituals and ceremonies of

Freemasonry, the new Grand Lodge styled itself 'The Antients' [sic] Grand Lodge'.

It was quick to attract new members and to grant authority to new lodges that adopted its rituals, and was soon rivalling the original Grand Lodge, now called in some quarters the Moderns' Grand Lodge.

By 1770, the Antients had chartered over 200 lodges, not just in London, but in the provinces and overseas as well. One of the reasons for their remarkable success was a series of tracts, the first one published in 1756 and entitled *Ahiman Rezon or a Help to a Brother* which set out the Antients' Constitutions, each edition more hostile in tone to the 'Moderns' than the one before. The tract was the work of Laurence Dermott, an Irish housepainter turned wine merchant who served the Antients' Grand Lodge as Grand Secretary for 20 years.

Dermott's highly readable style did much to attract would-be new members to the Antients' lodges, and their Grand Lodge became so respected in Scotland and Ireland that the Grand Lodges of both countries recognized it as the Freemasonic authority for English lodges.

The Moderns' Grand Lodge did not take this lying down. It continued to attract new members and to authorize new lodges that recognized its authority. Its success was in no short measure due to a book called *Illustrations of Masonry* by William Preston. First published in 1772, the book remained in print for almost 100 years. Its central thesis was that the principles of Freemasonry were more important than the petty feuds between Antients and Moderns, which to ordinary Masons seemed to be consuming more and more of the time of the grandees of both Grand Lodges.

When it came to religious tolerance, both Grand Lodges had reason to be proud. This was a time when Romanism was only just tolerated in an overwhelmingly Protestant country. It was an age when Catholics could not vote in general elections (they were not given the franchise until 1829) and were banned from holding many public offices. The anti-Romanism of establishment England did not stop Thomas Mathew in 1767 and Lord Petrie in 1772, proud Roman Catholics both, becoming Grand Master of the Antients and Moderns respectively.

Despite the differences between the two Grand Lodges, by the end of the eighteenth century Freemasonry was more and more regarded as a politically neutral, benevolent and tolerant institution, although this image was tarnished in the eyes of many by the events in France in 1789.

THE FRENCH REVOLUTION

On 4 July 1789 the Paris mob seized the Bastille in Paris, sparking off the French Revolution. (As a point of interest, the popular image of the Bastille being chock-full with political prisoners could not be further from the truth. When the Parisian rabble stormed the Bastille, it held a handful of captives and most of them were bankrupts, incarcerated for failure to pay their debts.) At first, the English were sympathetic to the ideals of the Revolution. An arrogant, tyrannical monarchy had been stripped of its power, which had been handed over to a democratic parliament of sorts.

Power eventually came to lie in the hands of a 'Committee of Public Safety', whose numbers included Danton, Robespierre and others, who, far from being the 'working-class men' of popular imagination, were almost exclusively culled from the upper-middle and professional classes. Danton, for instance, found it expedient to change the spelling of his name from the aristocratic-sounding D'Anton to something more ordinary. Both he and his ally Robespierre were lawyers who had studied at one of the most exclusive *lycées* in Paris.

Sympathy for the Revolution in England was to turn to disgust when Robespierre wrested power from his former allies and sent them and countless aristocrats (and the servants and retainers of noble families) to the guillotine during the Reign of Terror. And by a curious twist of circumstance, in England this disgust turned to anger against Freemasonry. The Revolution's slogan, '*Liberté, Egalite, Fraternite*' sounded suspiciously like the ideals of Brotherly Love that Freemasons held dear. Somehow the idea that Freemasons were responsible for the Reign of Terror

took hold for a short time, during which it was dangerous to admit to being a member of a lodge, either Antient or Modern.

Fortunately, this anti-Masonic hysteria was short-lived and Freemasonry was soon restored in the eyes of most sensible people as a patriotic organization, loyal to God and the Crown. So much so that when the Unlawful Societies Act (a late eighteenth century equivalent of a twenty-first century counter-terrorism measure) was passed in 1799, Freemasonry was exempted from the measure.

THE ARTICLES OF UNION

As the nation came together to fight first the War of the French Revolution (during which the fledgling United States of America repaid the assistance that the French had given them during the American War of Independence) and then the Napoleonic Wars, so the Antients and the Moderns decided to bury the hatchet. In 1798, the Moderns made the first tentative moves to come to some sort of agreement with the rival Grand Lodge. It took 15 years of careful negotiation before a document that covered the concerns of all (or most) was drawn up. It was not until December 1813 that the Articles of Union, twenty-one in all, was signed by the officials of both Grand Lodges and a single body was created as the premier authority regarding all things Freemasonic in England – the United Grand Lodge of England.

The first Grand Master of the United Grand Lodge was one of George III's younger sons, Augustus Frederick, the Duke of Sussex. The duke was a scholarly man with a deep interest in theology. Not unlike the present Prince of Wales, his views were on occasion the subject of mockery from his less intellectual brothers. He held a deep and sincere belief in political and religious tolerance. Not only was he outspoken in his belief in Catholic emancipation, but he counted several leading Jews among his circle, this in a time when anti-Semitism was if not open, then always bubbling beneath the surface.

Sussex set about trying to put his beliefs into action, determined to make The Craft more accessible to non-Christians. Whatever his religion might be, as long as a man was sincere in it, and as long as he lived his life by a decent moral code, that, according to the duke's way of thinking, should be enough.

Augustus Frederick wanted The Craft to be open to men of all faiths. 'Let a man's religion or mode of worship be what it may,' he wrote, 'he is not excluded from the Order provided he believe in a glorious architect of heaven and practise the sacred duties of morality.'

It was his influence and persuasive argument that resulted, within 20 or so years of the United Grand Lodge coming into being, in all references to Christianity being removed from Craft rituals, thereby allowing non-Christians to seek admittance to a lodge without in any way compromising their religious beliefs.

As Laurence Dermott had written in the Antients' Constitution, Freemasonry became (80 or more years after he penned the words) 'the centre of the union between good men and true, and the happy means of conciliating friendship among those who must otherwise have remained at a perpetual distance'.

The work of Augustus Frederick and other like-minded men reinvigorated Freemasonry. Any remnants of the suspicion with which it had been held during the French Revolution had evaporated. The days when The Craft was seen by many as little more than a social club (albeit one whose members were encouraged to live by a basic moral code) were gone. The English Craft rituals as revised by the duke and others focused on the fact that Brotherly Love, Relief and Truth were central to the movement, along with belief that God (be it the Roman Catholic God, the Protestant God, the Jewish God, whichever God or whichever pantheon) was central to human existence on earth.

It was this that gave Freemasonry the strength not just to survive but to flourish at a time when other ersatz masonic organizations which lacked a strong central moral code faded and struggled to carry on. This was the gift of Frederick Augustus and his compatriots to the Craft, and today's members of the United Grand Lodge of England and its associate lodges are eternally grateful to them for it.

'Liberté Égalite Fraternité' – the demands of the French Revolutionaries. Some thought the slogan so similar to the ideals of Freemasonry that they blamed it for the Reign of Terror

James II flees for France after defeat at the Battle of the Boyne. The English government's treatment of him was a contributing factor to the distrust with which Catholic monarchs of Europe viewed Freemasonry

AROUND THE WORLD

The eighteenth century saw Freemasonry becoming established in the eyes of most Englishmen as a force for good, although, to be fair, it retained the aura of being a club for men of means and influence with a fair degree of self-help being evident. The same century saw The Craft spring into life in Europe and wherever European, particularly British, emigrants travelled in search of a new and better life. . .

The English Grand Lodge was founded at a time when it was the custom of upper-class young men (and some not so young, in a bid to recapture the joys of youth) to do the Grand Tour of Europe. They crossed the English Channel and headed for the capitals of the continent to soak themselves in culture and to buy furniture and furnishings for their grand houses back home. All of them took with them not just what they thought they would need for the journey, but news of the formation of the Grand Lodge, and by the end of the 1730s masonic lodges had been formed in Holland and throughout the Austrian Empire, Prussia, Italy, Spain and Sweden.

THE ENGLISH GRAND LODGE

Freemasonry was to prove popular abroad with men of the same sort as were initiated into the English lodges, but in countries where Roman Catholicism was the established religion, The Craft came to be regarded with suspicion by the governments there.

Less than 30 years before the English Grand Lodge had been established, the British had forced the Catholic James II to flee and replaced him as monarch with the Protestant William of Orange and his wife, Mary, both of whom had their own claim to the throne. William was a grandson of Charles I through his mother, Princess Mary. Mary was James' daughter by his first wife, Anne Hyde, who died before he acceded to the throne.

In the minds of many European governments, Freemasonry – a secret society with strong links to a constitutional monarchy – was something to be regarded with suspicion. The English lodges counted many of the nobility among their members. In 1688, the mainly Protestant English nobility had been at the forefront of the move to depose James. What would happen in Europe, some governments asked, if the English belief in constitutional monarchy came to influence, via Freemasonry, the political thinkers who lived in the absolute monarchies of France and other countries whose kings and emperors believed in the 'Divine Right' of monarchs to rule?

But strangely, the first anti-Freemason measures were taken not in one of the Catholic monarchies, but in Protestant Holland, where, in 1735, a proclamation was issued that stated that the 'so-called Fraternity of Freemasons' had formed an illegal association. The proclamation insisted that the real reason for the association was 'faction and debauchery'.

THE VATICAN'S VIEW

Freemasonry was denounced by two papal bulls and it was part of the Inqusition's work to investigate it for heresy and other charges

Three years after the Dutch proclamation, in April 1738 Pope Clement XII issued a papal bull in which he condemned Freemasonry as a movement in which men took oaths on the Bible to preserve the secrets of their societies. Why, Clement wanted to know, was there a need for such secrecy if the lodges' members were doing good (as they claimed) and not the evil of which many accused them? In the words of the bull, 'if such people were not doing evil they would never have so much hatred of the light'. Clement forbade Catholics to become Freemasons on pain of the bell, book and candle (excommunication), something that was reiterated 13 years later by a second papal bull that railed against Freemasonry, this one issued by Pope Benedict XIV.

Clement's bull shocked Freemasons in Italy where many lodges had been formed by Roman Catholic supporters of James II's son, the self-styled James III, the Old Pretender. But it was enforced throughout the papal states and in much of the rest of Italy.

In the Portuguese capital, Lisbon, a lodge which had been formed by émigré Irish Catholics, was dissolved immediately after its members heard of the bull. An investigation by the Inquisition (the arm of the Church that investigated claims of heresy) cleared the members of immorality, irreligion or disloyalty to king and state, but the lodge remained closed.

A year later in Spain, the lodge formed by the English lord the Duke of Wharton (later Northumberland) was dissolved when the bull was put into effect there.

BEYOND THE BULL

One country where the papal bulls had little or no influence on The Craft was Sweden, which had been staunchly Lutheran since the Reformation. In 1753, Count Carl Frederik Scheffer, who had been initiated while he was living in Paris in 1737, was elected Grand Master of the Lodge St Jean, which considered itself the Mother Lodge of Sweden, and thereby entitled to issue warrants to other lodges in the country. Despite his noble background, Scheffer was influential in introducing men from other classes in The Craft.

In 1756, Carl Frederik Eckleff and six fellow Freemasons formed the Scottish lodge *L'Innocent* in Stockholm, working the so-called Scottish St Andrew's degrees. Three years later, Eckleff established a Grand Chapter in the capital. In 1760 the Grand Lodge of Sweden was established, and was recognized 10 years later as a national Grand Lodge by the Grand Lodge of England.

The Swedish monarchy has always played an active role in The Craft there and, for more than 200 years, succeeding Swedish kings have served as Grand Master. Indeed it was a Swedish monarch who introduced Britain's Edward VII into The Craft when, as Prince of Wales, Edward was on an official visit to Stockholm in 1868.

In 1780 and again in 1800 Karl III revised the rituals of the Swedish Rite and established a Masonic system with several more degrees than the English model of Apprentice, Fellow Craft and Master Mason. (Prince Edward, incidentally, passed all the degrees of the Swedish Rite.) The top one in the Swedish Rite is now Most Enlightened Brother, Knight Commander of the Red Cross (the XIth Degree) of which there are around 60.

In 1811 Karl established the Royal Order of King Karl III, a civil order which, although not a Masonic degree, has a membership of only 33, all of whom must be Masons of the XIth degree.

The Swedish Rite is today worked all over Scandinavia and is unusual in that, whereas in most other countries Freemasons have to profess a belief in a Supreme Being, be it the Christian or Jewish God, or one of the Pantheon of other faiths and religions, in Sweden, Christianity is a prerequisite for membership of The Craft.

AN ARRESTING INCIDENT

In Austria, Vienna's first Freemasons' lodge was formed in 1742, later than in other parts of the Austro-Hungarian Empire. A year after it was established, police in the city were tipped off about a special meeting of the lodge at which 'distinguished foreign brothers' were to be present. The city's Roman Catholic chief of police, knowing that not only was Freemasonry a secret society whose members were sympathetic to Protestant Britain, but that it had been condemned by Clement XII, advised the empress, Maria Theresa, to authorize her soldiers to raid the premises and arrest whoever was there. The armed soldiers burst into the room, swords drawn, and arrested the twenty men meeting there. They included a German prince, a Bohemian count, an English viscount, a French aristocrat, several Austrian noblemen and a few members from the *bourgeoisie*.

King Edward VII (far right) attained all the degrees in the Swedish Rite and was also Grand Master of the United Grand Lodge of England from 1874 until he came to the throne in 1901

An early nineteenth century set design for The Magic Flute. *Musicologists can find ties with The Craft in the music as well as in the story*

The foreigners were promptly released. The upper-class Austrians were put under house arrest but their lower-class compatriots were incarcerated in the city jail where they languished for twelve days until they were freed under an amnesty authorized by Maria Theresa to commemorate her infant son's name day. She did, however, authorize very heavy penalties to be imposed should the lodge ever meet again. Its members were so relieved at being freed unpunished that they complied, not even formally meeting to dissolve their lodge.

Many years later, when writing about a painting of a scene from Mozart's opera *The Magic Flute* (see p. 124), an expert who had known the composer, said:

> *The wicked Queen of the Night, who persecutes the young hero, is Marie Theresa* [sic]. *The evil spirits who encourage her to do are the Catholic Church. The all-wise, just and beneficial ruler Sarastro, punishing the wicked and protecting the good, is Joseph II* [Maria Theresa's son in whose honour the Viennese Freemasons had been released] *or any other well-meaning autocrat who protected the Freemasons.*

'FLOREAT' FREEMASONRY

In the German states (of which there were so many – kingdoms, principalities, grand-duchies, duchies, counties palatine, electorates and margravates – that it was once remarked that there was one for every day of the year, including leap years) Freemasonry flourished. This was probably the result of having so many independently minded states and so many like-minded citizens. That said, there were many who were firmly against it, none more so than Frederick William, the first king of Prussia.

Frederick William may have been politically astute enough to convert the Duchy of Brandenburg, which he inherited in 1713, to the Kingdom of Prussia, which became the dominant, all-powerful German state under his own and his son's (Frederick the Great) rule, but he was a mentally unbalanced bully. So much so that when young Frederick tried to flee Prussia during military manoeuvres with his favourite, a young army officer called Katte, Frederick William had them arrested and tried for desertion by a court martial. Both men were sentenced to death. Frederick's sentence was commuted to life imprisonment, but his partner in 'crime' (and probably in bed) was beheaded in the courtyard that Frederick's cell overlooked. After the axe had fallen, Katte's head was held up for the young prince to see, whereupon he fainted.

A few years later in 1738, released, officially forgiven and restored to grudging paternal favour, Frederick and his father travelled to Holland where at a dinner

The Prussian monarch Frederick the Great was entered into Freemasonry in 1738 and remained loyal to the ideals of The Craft until his death in 1786

party in The Hague the conversation turned to Freemasonry. The Prussian king was so violent in his reaction against it that Frederick's support for it was meekly expressed in a few short words. However, he later confessed to his host, the Count van der Lippe-Buckenburg, that he would like to be entered, but, given his father's violent hatred of The Craft, it would have to be done without the older man knowing anything about it.

The count arranged for Frederick to be initiated at Brunswick, on the royal progress back to Berlin. When members of the lodge gathered in the hotel where the ritual was to take place, they realized that they could easily be heard in the next room, where a Hanoverian nobleman was resident. Fearful that he would understand what was happening and that word of the secret initiation would find its way back to Frederick William, members of the lodge called one by one on the man, whose weakness for wine, and his low tolerance of it, were well known, to pay their respects. Mindful of his duties as a host, the Hanoverian offered each of his guests in turn a glass and partook of one himself. As a result, as Prince William was initiated into The Craft, there was a very drunken upper-class German slumped comatose on his bed in the next room.

Frederick William died two years later, to be succeeded by his son, who was to become one of the most powerful rulers in Europe, and a Freemason. Frederick was many things. He was a brilliant military tactician and commander who enjoyed music and philosophy, and in politics and religion he was a man of liberal views. And he was a devoted lover of all things French.

THE CRAFT IN FRANCE

The first Masonic lodges were warranted in France perhaps as long ago as 1725, when the monarch Louis XV, like all his Bourbon predecessors an absolute ruler if ever there was one, was on the throne. Although there was a nominal system of devolved government in the country, with each district being governed by an *intendant*, whose authority within their area was absolute, each *intendant* was subject to the *surintendants*, and the *surintendants* to the King's Council, which was very much the *King's* Council. He could accept or reject as he pleased any advice given to him.

Even papal bulls had little or no authority in France. Although Louis styled himself the most Christian of kings, he did not allow the Church in France to become too subservient to Rome. It may have been a *Roman* Catholic Church, but Louis saw to it that it served the *French* state.

Louis enjoyed an ambivalent relationship with members of the French nobility, who, through seigniorial courts, exercised jurisdiction over their tenants. But the decisions of these courts could be overturned on appeal to the king's courts. In exchange for their loyalty, Louis continued the tradition whereby the aristocracy paid no tax.

As the eighteenth century ran its course, more and more Frenchmen, including members of the aristocracy, many of whom had joined Freemasonic lodges started to question this privilege and it was more than likely that it was the subject of much discussion at lodge meetings.

Louis had no objection to the nobility becoming Freemasons. But the middle classes? That was quite another story. There was no way that Louis would countenance them joining what was in effect a secret society that could start questioning the *status quo*. And so, in 1737, a few months before Clement denounced Freemasonry in his bull, *In Eminenti*, Louis banned Freemasonry in France.

Despite the ban, and despite the fact that Louis had decreed that any nobleman who joined a lodge would not be received at court and would consequently be rendered ineligible for any of the prequisites that court life could afford Freemasonry continued to flourish in France, where the Grand lodge was known as *La Grande Loge Anglais*.

Freemasonry in France differed from the English brotherhood. There were several Grand Lodges and countless councils, rites and chapters. Some of them vanished only to be revived a few years later. Others combined, with members

The banner of French Grand Lodge No. 554. The symbols it shows will be as familiar to Freemasons today as it was to those alive when it was embroidered in the nineteenth century

A candidate is led towards the Book during a 33rd Degree ceremony. To reach this stage, the candidate must have passed several degrees. Only then can he be a candidate for the 33rd – Inspector General of the Supreme Council

unhappy with the union establishing splinter organizations of their own. At one time, the 34 Masonic Orders contained somewhere between 1,400 and 1,500 degrees. Some of these were 'Lodges of Adoption' meetings conducted by a regular lodge at which women were admitted.

In England the three degrees – Entered Apprentice, Fellow Craft and Master Mason – were inviolate. And Freemasonry was a male bastion.

Most of the extra degrees that existed in French (and German) Freemasonry at the time were linked with chivalric legends and such organizations as the Knights Templar, and the rituals they involved were much more elaborate than the simple English ones. Perhaps it was the fact that most, if not all, French Masons were Roman Catholics and consequently had been imbued with a love of colourful church pageantry that accounted for their grand masonic ritual. And perhaps it was their love of grand titles that attracted French aristocrats to the numerous degrees. At a time when marquises and counts were ten a penny in France, to be a Prince of Jerusalem or Grand Inspector Inquisitor had a certain cachet.

THE ANCIENT SCOTTISH RITE

The various degrees and grades of French Freemasonry at the time were linked by their respect for *L'Ecossais* or Scottish degrees, which derive from what is known as the Ramsay Orations. Andrew Ramsay, also known as the Chevalier de Ramsay, was a Scots-born Freemason who talked of Freemasonry as having arisen in the Holy Land during the Crusades as an order of Chivalry.

In 1728 he proposed to the English Grand Lodge that the three degrees of Apprentice, Fellow Craft and Master be replaced with three degrees of his own invention – Scotch Mason, Novice and Knight of the Temple. The Grand Lodge was not amused.

It was a different story in France. He took his three degrees there and they became so popular, eventually giving rise to a total of 33 in all, that they have since become known as The Ancient Scottish Rite *or L'Ecossais.*

Among lodges following *L'Ecossais* were The Chapter of Clermont with seven degrees, founded in 1750 by the Chevalier de Bonneville; the Rite of St Martin, which was founded by the Marquis de St Martin in 1767; the Illuminati of Avignon, which was introduced into Paris by a Benedictine monk and a Polish baron in 1760; and numerous others. And, determined that the ladies should not be left out, in the years before the French Revolution broke out in 1789, a certain Madame de Chaumont founded the Knights and Nymphs of the Rose in Paris as an Adoptive Order into which women could be initiated.

These orders were mostly founded independent of one another, but by 1760 an organized Ancient Scottish Rite had been established under the control of the Grand Lodge of France, also known as The Grand Orient.

When Louis XV died in 1774, the throne passed to his grandson, whose father had died some years earlier. Louis XVI was as weak as his grandfather had been strong. His reign was marked by financial crisis after financial crisis. Despite them, Louis continued to reward his favourites and their families with generous pensions, and his wife, Maria Theresa's daughter Marie Antoinette, flaunted her extravagant spending in the faces of the French people who had adored her when she first arrived in France from Austria to marry Prince Louis.

REVOLUTION AND EMPIRE

In 1788, Louis was forced to summon a meeting of the States-General, the French 'parliament' that had last met in 1614! It was made up of representatives of the Church (the First Estate), the aristocracy (the Second Estate) and middle-class men of property (the Third Estate).

It wasn't long before the Third Estate challenged the right of the other two to have any say in France's government and proclaimed itself to be *the* National Assembly and assumed legislative power.

Louis, whose cousin, the influential Duke of Orleans, was to become a leading member of the Assembly, lacked the authority to influence things and did next to

nothing to stop what was happening. But when a rumour spread in Paris that he was planning to dissolve the Assembly and arrest its leaders, the mob stormed the Bastille, an event seen by many as the start of the French Revolution proper.

In 1793, five years after the storming of the Bastille, Louis was put on trial charged with plotting with Austrian and other armies that were invading France. When he was found guilty, the Assembly, now self-styled the Convention, voted by a majority of seventy-one to execute him. A resolution that the sentence be postponed was defeated by one vote. Among those who voted for the sentence to be carried out was Orleans, now called Philippe Egalité, who had been Grand Master of the French Grand Orient (Grand Lodge).

Enemies of The Craft claimed that Freemasons had been responsible for the Revolution, and it is probably true that many members of the Assembly and Convention were, and had been, lodge members (one estimate has it that out of 1,336 delegates, 320 [24 per cent] were Freemasons). And it could be said that, given the single vote majority not to postpone Louis' execution and that Philippe Egalité had voted against the motion, it was his vote that had sent his cousin to the guillotine. Those who hold this view are no doubt happy that Philippe followed Louis to the guillotine a few months later.

It was Freemasonry's reputation for attracting upper-class and aristocratic men into its numbers that was responsible for its decline in France during the Revolu-

Contrary to popular myth, there were only a handful of prisoners in the Bastille when it was stormed. Nonetheless this event sparked off the French Revolution

tion. By the time Louis and his cousin lost their heads to Madame la Guillotine (whose eponymous inventor was himself a member of a lodge), it had more or less vanished. It reappeared with Napoleon's rise to power.

Napoleon, like many absolute rulers, was suspicious of any secret organization, but after he came to power there was a revival in The Craft, despite his disregard for it. He felt that lodge meetings might be a front for opposition to his regime and decreed that government consent had to be obtained before any regular meetings of more than twenty people could be held for religious, political or other objectives.

Although Freemasons eventually gained imperial consent to continue with their lodge meetings, the emperor ordered his interior minister to investigate whether or not they were involved in any political activities. The only area of the French Empire where Napoleon's prefects found any evidence of disloyal Freemasons was in Geneva, which French troops had occupied in 1798. The rest of his Freemason subjects were judged to be loyal citizens. Among them, although not a Freemason *per se* was Napoleon's first wife, Josephine, who was Grand Mistress of the Saint Caroline Lodge of Adoption.

Elsewhere in Europe during the French Revolution and its aftermath, Freemasonry enjoyed mixed fortunes. In countries where Catholic monarchs feared the spread of the revolutionary principles of 'Liberty, Equality and Fraternity' it was banned and suppressed. In other countries, men were free to join a lodge without fear of any untoward consequences.

In the years following the Napoleonic Wars, and with the increasing democratization of the continent shown by the revolutions that broke out in several countries in 1830 and 1848, Freemasonry flourished, no more so than in France. In 1830, Louis XVI's Bourbon cousin was deposed in favour of Philippe Egalité's son, Louis Philippe, who in turn was deposed in 1848 and eventually replaced by Napoleon's nephew, who assumed the title of emperor in 1851. (French politics is nothing if not incestuous!)

Napoleon III was acutely interested in Freemasonry, but for political rather than altruistic or philosophical reasons. Aware of the precariousness of his position, he kept a close watch on any group that might conceivably be discussing alternative leaders or alternative systems of government. He even went as far as imposing his own candidate for Grand Master of the Grand Orient of France, although he subsequently restored to the members the right to select their own Grand Master.

Napoleon himself was deposed after he had been captured by the Prussian army during the Battle of Sedan, in 1870. Freemasons played a prominent part in the ensuing revolution, the Paris Commune and the civil war between the government and the Commune.

The emperor's exile (spent in the quiet English country town of Chislehurst in Kent) ushered in an anti-clerical, anti-religious era in France, especially in Paris, where the communists remained influential even after the Commune was abolished. So strong was the anti-religious feeling that the Grand Orient

The French emperor, Napoleon III, surrenders to the Prussian kaiser in 1870 after defeat at the Battle of Sedan

decreed that a professed belief in a Supreme Being was no longer a prerequisite for membership. Now open to agnostics, atheists and freethinkers, the Grand Orient scratched out any mention of God from both its rituals and its constitution and went as far as removing the Bible from all lodges and abolishing the practice of candidates for admission taking their oaths on the sacred book of whichever religion they belonged to.

Masons in other countries were appalled, even more so when the Grand Orient decided that it would now involve itself in active politics, especially in social affairs. So strong was the feeling that it was given an ultimatum by the other Grand Lodges: either it should return to its old ways or face a future as outcasts in world Freemasonry.

The French, as the French so often do, refused to recant, and until 1913, when the National Grand Lodge of France was constituted, the Grand Orient was regarded as 'an irregular body' by the Grand Lodges of every other country.

THE TWENTIETH CENTURY

The last 100 years has seen the rise of left- and right-wing totalitarian regimes in many countries in Europe, and the continent has twice been a battlefield. Freemasonry has suffered accordingly, being seen by suspicious dictators as involved in anti-government political activities.

In Russia, the ban on The Craft imposed by the reactionary Alexander I in 1822 continued until 1917, when, following the Revolution, Alexander Kerensky, the democratic leader and a Mason, let the ban lapse and a Grand Lodge was established in the Ukraine. But not for long. Within a few months the Communists seized power, Freemasonry was banned, and when the Ukraine was absorbed into the USSR, its fledging Grand Lodge was suppressed.

The end of the First World War brought with it the break up of the Austro-Hungarian Empire, which had controlled much of Central Europe for centuries. Although a Grand Lodge had been established in Hungary in 1870, Freemasonry had been banned in Austria since 1794. With the establishment of an Austrian Republic in 1918, the ban was lifted and a Grand Lodge duly formed. Grand Lodges also appeared in other parts of the old empire, including Romania and Czechoslovakia.

The end of the First World War also saw the start of the eventual rise to power of right-wing dictatorships in other parts of the continent. Within 15 years or so of the 1918 Armistice, in Mussolini's Italy, Franco's Spain, Salazar's Portugal and Hitler's Germany, all opposition and suspected opposition, which included The Craft, was suppressed, and nowhere more so than in Nazi Germany.

The Franco-Prussian War of 1870–1 had been the final stage in the unification of Germany, which transformed the loose alliance of a multitude of independent states that existed in the seventeenth and eighteenth centuries into a European superpower under Prussian leadership. Many of these states had had their own Grand Lodges, and even after a unified German state was established, no attempt was made to establish a unified Grand Lodge.

After Germany's defeat in the First World War, a document called *The Protocols of the Learned Elders of Zion* was circulated. People who read it were horrified by what they read: it described nothing less than a plot by a group of Jews and Freemasons to achieve world domination. The document was a crude forgery, but that did not stop other equally absurd publications being given widespread credence.

In 1933, Hitler's Nazi Party came to power and used the anti-Semitic and anti-Masonic fervour stirred up by the *Protocols* and other pamphlets to help him band the German people behind him. Hitler's argument that Freemasons and Jews had colluded in taking over Germany and had brought the country to its economic knees struck a cord with the man in the German street who had seen the Reichsmark tumble in value.

The hellish ordeal of the Jews in Hitler's Germany remains, 70 years on, a stain on the world's conscience, but Nazism's attitude towards Freemasonry is not so well known. The various Grand Lodges were closed down, their records and regalia being seized by the all-powerful Nazis. Freemasons were barred from joining the armed forces and Masons already serving in them were removed from their duties. So, too, were Masons who were members of the Civil Service.

After the Second World War broke out, Freemasons in Norway, Finland, Denmark, Holland, Belgium, France, Greece, Luxembourg, Poland, Czechoslovakia, Hungary, Greece, Austria and Romania – everywhere Hitler's men were in control – suffered in the same way as their German fellow Masons had in pre-war Germany. Many non-Jewish Masons met the same fate as their Jewish brothers in the

The German pamphlet that accused Jews and Freemasons of plotting to dominate the world. The pamphlet was used by Hitler to unite public opinion behind the Nazis

73

concentration camps of the Third Reich. A conservative estimate puts the number gassed at 80,000, another at 200,000: a mere fraction of the millions of Jews who perished but a terrible toll all the same.

From a distance of more than 70 years, it is hard for us to comprehend how the Nazis got it away with it. The answer, one can only suppose, is fear: the fear of the ordinary man in the German street that if they did not go along with what was happening, then they, too, would meet the same fate.

But The Craft survived and with the Allies' victory was quick to re-establish itself in the countries that had been occupied by the Germans. And in Germany, too, by the beginning of 1946 plans were afoot to revive Freemasonry under the auspices of a unified Grand Lodge.

Sadly, this was not to be the case in much of Central and Eastern Europe. Within a few years of the break-up of the Austro-Hungarian Empire, the new democracies in which Grand Lodges had been established were overrun by Nazi troops and The

Craft suppressed. When the Second World War came to an end, these countries found themselves satellite states of Stalin's Russia and their fledgling Masonic lodges proscribed.

Today, with the break-up of the USSR and the re-establishment of democratic governments throughout the old Soviet empire, Freemasons are again free to meet in their lodges, to go through their rituals and practise their ideals.

Today, from Finland in the north to Greece in the south, from the Atlantic coast in the west to the Ural Mountains in the east, in every country of Europe The Craft of Freemasonry flourishes as a force for good in a troubled world.

ALL POINTS EAST AND WEST

The seventeenth, eighteenth and nineteenth centuries witnessed the age of European expansionism with the United Kingdom, France and Holland (first in the race)

Portuguese officials land at Timor, in Indonesia in 1820. In most of the places they colonized, European settlers established lodges where they could meet, discuss matters of mutual interest – and enjoy the pleasures of the Festive Board

vying with each other to carve themselves empires in Asia, Africa and the New World. (The Spanish and the Portuguese had already divided much of Central and South America up between themselves and by and large 'new' Europe left the 'old' European colonies unaffected by its imperial rivalries.)

Freemasonry proved to be extremely attractive to the independent-minded English colonists of North America and had an enormous effect on the founding of the United States, something we will look at in more detail in the next chapter.

During the Napoleonic era, French masons founded lodges all round the Mediterranean in parts of Africa and in the Caribbean. Lodges were established by Dutch masons in the Dutch East Indies and in Holland's colonies in Central and South America. And with the expansion of the British Empire into all points north, south, east and west, ex-patriots from the United Kingdom founded lodges loyal to the English, Scottish and Irish constitutions in places as far apart as Accra and Wellington.

THE CRAFT IN AFRICA

It was only nine years after the English Grand Lodge had been formed that a Freemason called Richard Hull was granted a patent by the Grand Lodge to style himself Grand Master for the Gambia, in West Africa. For reasons unknown to us, he never made use of the patent and as far as we know, he never realized his plans to found a Gambian Grand Lodge.

But Freemasonry was eventually to prove popular all over West Africa, lodges following the traditions of whichever European country first colonized them. If that happened to be Britain, then the men who settled there and took their Masonic traditions with them could have been English, Scottish or Irish (no discourtesy is intended to the Welsh, who, in matters Freemasonic, tend to follow the English tradition). Which is why in Nigeria and Ghana there are lodges of English, Irish and Scottish constitution. Other West African countries, Gabon, the Ivory Coast and Liberia, have independent Grand Lodges. In Benin, Senegal and other West African countries that were once French territories Freemasonry is mainly commissioned by the Grand Orient.

German Freemasonry is also evident in the area but only a little. Germany came late to the empire game, her imperial ambitions only born with the unification of the German states in 1870, by which time Britain and France (and Holland) had divided much of the continent between them. Togo, which was part of the German empire from the 1880s until the end of the First World War, when it was ceded to Britain and France, has German lodges, as well as those commissioned by the British Grand Lodges and the Grand Orient.

There is a German influence at the other side of the continent, too, in Tanzania, which, as Tanganyika, was once ruled from Berlin. Further north, in Egypt, which was part of the Turkish Ottoman Empire, a Grand Lodge was formed in 1864. Before that there were lodges of Greek, Italian and French origin, the French having been particularly active in the country during Napoleon's rule.

France was also the dominant European influence in northern Africa and French lodges were formed there. Some still meet, but with the rise of Islamic fundamentalism in North Africa, Freemasonry has now been banned in several countries.

Holland was the first European country to colonize South Africa, and Dutch settlers established lodges loyal to the Dutch Grand Lodge in the late eighteenth century. They were followed by the British, who formed lodges commissioned from home, the first being an English one in 1811.

THE INDIAN SUB-CONTINENT

Meanwhile, across the Indian Ocean, many Britons had settled in the sub-continent serving in the British army, working for the Indian Civil Service or the East India Company. It was only natural that those men who had been lodge members back home took their Freemasonry with them, and by 1730 a lodge had been founded in

Calcutta, followed over the next few years by others in Madras and Bombay.

At first these were solely the territory of ex-patriot Europeans, but it was not long before ambitious Indians wanting to emulate the Europeans that they admired so much were showing an interest in The Craft. This was opposed by some lodge members, who held that the Hindu pantheon made it impossible for them to declare their belief in one single Supreme Being, a prerequisite of acceptance into a lodge.

The problem was put before the Grand Master of the English Grand Lodge back in Britain, the Duke of Sussex. He declared that a Mason's religion was his own business and that the gods in whom the Hindus believed were various personifications of the one Supreme Being. The way was open for Dr George Burns, Provincial Grand Master for Western India and one of the men who had argued for the admission of Indians, to found a lodge in Bombay, commissioned by the Grand Lodge of Scotland, that was open to the local population. It wasn't just Hindus who were

A viceregal lodge in India. Many of the British men who served in India, were members of lodges 'back home' and it was only natural that they took The Craft with them when they sailed for the sub-continent

accepted in The Craft in India – by the time the sub-continent was given independence in 1947, Muslims, Parsees and Sikhs had been admitted to lodges all over India.

This racial and social equality engendered by Freemasonry in India was summed up by Rudyard Kipling, a loyal Freemason who lived in India from 1880-89, and who wrote in his poem *The Mother Lodge*:

> *Outside – Sergeant! Sir, Salute! Salaam!*
> *Inside – Brother and it don't do no 'arm.*
> *We met upon the Level, and we parted on the Square,*
> *An' was Junior Deacon in my Mother-Lodge out there.*
> *We'd Bola Nath, Accountant,*
> *An' Saul the Aden Jew,*
> *An' Din Mohammed, draughtsman*
> *Of the Survey Office, too.*
> *There was Babu Chuckerbutty,*
> *An' Amir Singh the Sikh,*
> *An' Castro from the fittin'-sheds,*
> *The Roman Catholik!*

With independence in 1947, many Britons left for home and 14 years later the Grand Lodge of India was founded. With independence, too, came the division of the sub-continent into Hindu India and Muslim Pakistan. Whereas The Craft has continued to flourish in India, in Pakistan it has been suppressed by the Islamic government.

FREEMASONRY IN THE FAR EAST

Freemasonry also suffered under Islam in other parts of Asia. And in China it was banned in 1949 by the Communists, although the Grand Lodge of China continues to govern The Craft in Taiwan, while in Hong Kong (now a self-governing part of China) there are lodges loyal to the English, Scottish and Irish constitutions.

Among the many Englishmen who sailed to Asia to seek his fortune in the nineteenth century was Thomas Stamford Raffles who joined the East India Company when he was a boy. When he was 24 he was appointed assistant secretary to the governor of Penang and by 1811 he had risen to the rank of lieutenant-governor of Java where he was initiated into Freemasonry by the Master of the Lodge there, the former Dutch governor of the island.

Eight years later he bought the island of Singapore for the East India Company, whereupon, true to the ideas of his Craft, he declared it a free port 'open to ships of every nation'. Thanks to that vision, it is today one of the most prosperous countries in Asia and one with a significant Masonic presence.

IN THE ANTIPODES

Much further to the east, is Australia, where the first 'settlers' were convicts from Britain and had little opportunity to form lodges, even if they had wanted to. But by the beginning of the nineteenth century, more conventional settlers sailed to the antipodes in search of wealth and a new life, and Freemasonry began to establish itself there. The early years were not without excitement, for in 1803, after one of the first meetings, the men present were arrested on orders of the Governor of New South Wales, who believed the meeting constituted an illegal gathering. Happily, the fledging Australian Freemasons were soon released and more lodges began to be commissioned.

As more Europeans arrived, more and more land was settled and the individual states which today form the Commonwealth of Australia began to be established, and one by one Grand Lodges came into being in each state. South Australia was first, in 1884, followed four years later by New South Wales. Grand Lodges were formed in Victoria in 1889, in Tasmania in 1890 and in Western Australia (where,

The mix of men mentioned in Rudyard Kipling's poem The Mother Lodge *shows the breadth of membership of the Indian lodges*

Simon Bolivar victorious at the Battle of Carabobo in 1821. Bolivar entered The Craft when he was a young man and although he remained true to its ideals, his autocratic manner made him unpopular

during the 1890s the population was swelled by prospectors in search of gold) in 1899. The last state to form a Grand Lodge was Queensland in the east of the country where squabbles between local lodges there were not settled until 1921.

Freemasons in Australia play an important part in the social life of the communities, not just giving to charities like their brethren in other parts of the world, but playing an active part in community activities and often being the first to offer practical help whenever it is needed.

So, too, do the Freemasons of New Zealand, where the first lodge was founded in 1842. A Grand Lodge for the whole country was established in 1890, but many New Zealand lodges decided to remain loyal to their own District Grand Lodges or to one of the UK traditions.

AN ANCIENT CRAFT IN A NEW WORLD

Centuries before European settlers sailed east to colonize Australia and later New Zealand, Portuguese and Spaniards had sailed west to the New World, at first in search of gold, and later in search of new land to farm and rear cattle. They converted many of the local population to Roman Catholicism and as good Catholics themselves many of them paid heed to the papal bulls that did much to suppress The Craft in their native countries.

But when liberation from rule from Lisbon and Madrid came, Freemasonry began to make its presence felt. Indeed, the man who liberated much of South America from European dominance, Simón Bolivar, was himself a Mason. He joined The Craft when he was living in Cadiz in Spain in the early years of the nineteenth century, and in 1807 he entered the Scottish Rite when he was staying in Paris. (For good measure, he also joined The Knights Templar the same year.)

In 1811 rebels in Venezuela, Bolivar among them, declared themselves independent of Spanish rule. The revolt failed and he was forced to flee to neighbouring New Grenada (present-day Colombia). Two years later, he rallied an army of 500 men to his side, led them into Venezuela and marched into Caracas, declaring 'war to the death' on the Spanish rulers and himself dictator of the western part of the country.

In 1814 he was driven out by royalist troops and retreated to the West Indies from where he made repeated attempts to retake Venezuela. Civil war raged in the area and it was not until 1821 that the rebels' victory at the Battle of Carabobo more or less ended the war, although Spanish patriots carried on a guerrilla war until 1824 when they were finally driven out of the country.

1821 saw Bolivar, 'The Liberator', being elected president of the Republic of Colombia, which then comprised Venezuela, Colombia and New Grenada. A year later he added Ecuador to the republic. In 1824 he drove the Spaniards out of Peru, making himself dictator there for a time, creating a separate state of Upper Peru, which was called Bolivia in his honour.

His autocratic manner and the unpopular constitution he tried to impose on Bolivia were responsible for his troops being driven from the fledgling state by dissident citizens of the new republic. Returning to Colombia in 1828, he assumed supreme power, something that caused so much apprehension in Venezuela that it separated itself from the republic in 1829. This in turn led Bolivar to quit office the following year, and he died a few months later.

Bolivar's life embodied the strength which is one of the Ideals of Freemasonry, and The Craft was to prove popular in the territory over which he ruled. Several subsequent presidents of Venezuela, Peru and Colombia were Freemasons, as have been the leaders of other South American countries including Uruguay and El Salvador.

At the same time that Bolivar and his rebels were fighting off Spanish rule in the north and west of South America, the flame of independence from European rule was burning just as fiercely in Portuguese territories in the east and south. In 1821, the year that saw Bolivar victorious at Carabobo, the prince regent of Brazil declared Brazil an independent empire and himself Pedro I. Pedro, like Bolivar, was a Freemason.

Now as then, despite the fact that South and Central America are predominantly strongly Roman Catholic countries, Freemasonry continues to attract members and there are lodges throughout each country in the area, all loyal to the virtues and ideals of The Craft.

IDEALS AND VIRTUES

But to round off this look at the development of Freemasonry in various parts of the world, let us return across the Atlantic to Africa, for it was in South Africa that The Craft's ideals and virtues were evidenced by an event that happened in 1977. The laws of Apartheid made it virtually impossible for white and coloured to meet together. But in that year the Grand Lodge of South Africa sought exemption from the law so that two lodges whose members were exclusively black could be admitted to full membership. In doing so, its members showed Strength and Wisdom – two of the three ideals – and Tolerance, Achievement, Charity, Integrity and Fidelity – all of the Five Virtues.

*The Capitol Building in Washington DC. One of the symbols of the United States,
it was designed and built by Freemasons*

CROSSING THE ATLANTIC

The men who sailed across the Atlantic to settle in the New World

brought many of their customs and practices along – among them

Freemasonry . . .

lthough there is no written record of Freemasonry in North America before the establishment of the English Grand Lodge in 1717, it is quite possible that the Masonic tradition crossed the Atlantic with the first English settlers in the seventeenth century, and that lodges were founded then. We do not know for certain.

BEFORE INDEPENDENCE

It is said that the earliest known American Freemason was Jonathan Belcher, who became Governor General of Massachusetts and New Hampshire in 1730. Born in Boston and educated at Harvard, Belcher made the crossing to England in the early years of the eighteenth century. Around 1704 he was, he claimed, introduced into a lodge in London. He returned to America in 1705, became a wealthy merchant and, later, a leading light in Freemasonry.

We don't know if these dates are accurate: they derive from a letter Belcher wrote in 1741 when he claimed to have been a Mason for 37 years. We do know, however, that when the new Americans learned that the foundation of the Grand Lodge had made Freemasonry fashionable in England among the top echelons of society, they became keen to emulate their English contemporaries and found lodges of their own.

According to historians of the premier (English) Grand Lodge, we can be absolutely certain that Freemasonry had been established in the American colonies by 1730, for records dating from that year tell that one Daniel Coxe was appointed as Grand Master for New York. In 1733, Henry Price was appointed Grand Master for New England and set about commissioning lodges in Boston and in other parts of the colony.

The oldest known American lodge on record is in St. John's Philadelphia, which had been commissioned by 1731 when Benjamin Franklin was initiated into The Craft. Franklin, the American statesman and scientist who was an active participant in the talks and meetings that resulted in the Declaration of Independence of 1776, probably became familiar with Freemasonry when he visited England at the age of 18 in 1724. Three years after he had been initiated at the Tun Tavern in Philadelphia, he became master of the lodge.

In 1734, Franklin, a printer by trade, published an American edition of James Anderson's *Constitutions* of 1723. Franklin was also a canny businessman and would not have done such a thing had he not known there would be a demand for the book. So we can be fairly certain that Freemasonry had been quick to establish itself in the North American colonies, attracting many men to the various lodges that were being commissioned at the time. Franklin's edition has the words, 'Reprinted by B. Franklin in the year of Masonry 5734. Price stitch'd at 2s 6d [12.5p], bound 4s [20p].'

The speed with which The Craft established itself in North America was probably due to the formation of military lodges by redcoats of the British Army who had been sent to the colonies. (The first record we have of military lodges date from 1641 when Sir Robert Moray, quarter-master general of a Scottish army that had occupied Newcastle-upon-Tyne was initiated into The Craft by some fellow soldiers whose Mother Lodge was in Edinburgh.)

After its creation in 1713, the Grand Lodge had approved the establishment of military lodges, which moved from place to place with the regiments who had founded them. Before one could be established, the approval of the commanding officer had to be sought and approved, and it was within his power to close it down if he wanted to. But as the commanding officer was more often than not a member, such a move was rare.

As membership of a military lodge was also in the patronage of the commanding officer, most of whom were 'gentlemen' whose families purchased their commissions and who considered that fraternization between officers and other ranks was bad for discipline, military lodges tended to be officer-only.

All the military lodges, including overseas ones, were commissioned by the Grand Lodge in London, and it exercised control over them via Provincial Grand Masters. It was Grand Lodge policy that these lodges were exclusively soldier-only, but the Provincial Grand Masters often waived this rule, allowing local gentry to be initiated into the military lodges. When the regiment was posted elsewhere, the civilian members left behind continued to attend lodge meetings, more often than not asking the Grand Lodge (again via the Provincial Grand Master) to constitute them as a new lodge affiliated to London.

British regiments were stationed all over the Atlantic seaboard, moving from place to place regularly. One month may have seen them finishing a tour of duty in Nova Scotia before marching south to relieve another one about to sail for home from a port in South Carolina. So the number of 'civilian' lodges grew rapidly throughout the colony. And as the non-military members of the lodges tended to be gentleman farmers or wealthy businessmen, they tended to attract new members from the same station.

As in England, there were those Freemasons to whom lodge meetings were events where philosophical, intellectual discussions could be enjoyed and views expressed and argued over, and there were others for whom The Craft was a vehicle for enjoyable social gatherings, good victuals, good wine and good fellowship. Benjamin Franklin belonged to the first category. Another famous American belonged to the second.

This tall, slave-owning, smartly dressed young man was initiated in The Craft at Fredericksburg in Virginia in 1752 and raised to Master Mason early the following year. His interest in surveying led him to be appointed by the Virginia government to look at the lie of the land on the border of Virginia and neighbouring Ohio, the beginnings of 'The West'. When war broke out between Britain and France, who had vast territories in America, he was given a commission in the British Army in 1756 and was eventually appointed head of the Virginia forces. We don't know if, at this time, his name ever came to the ears of the then British monarch, George II, but he was certainly known to George III. The loyal colonial officer was none other than George Washington.

THE FREEMASONS AND A FAMOUS PARTY

On 16 December 1773, three shipments of tea were thrown overboard from the holds of three British schooners lying at anchor in Boston Harbour by a party of men disguised as Native Americans. By a strange coincidence, a meeting of the St Andrew's Lodge closed early that evening as few members were present. The letter 'T' is written with tremendous flourish several times on the relevant page in the minute book, forever linking Freemasonry and one of the most famous events in US history – the Boston Tea Party.

The colonists' anger was the result of the fact that although they paid taxes to the

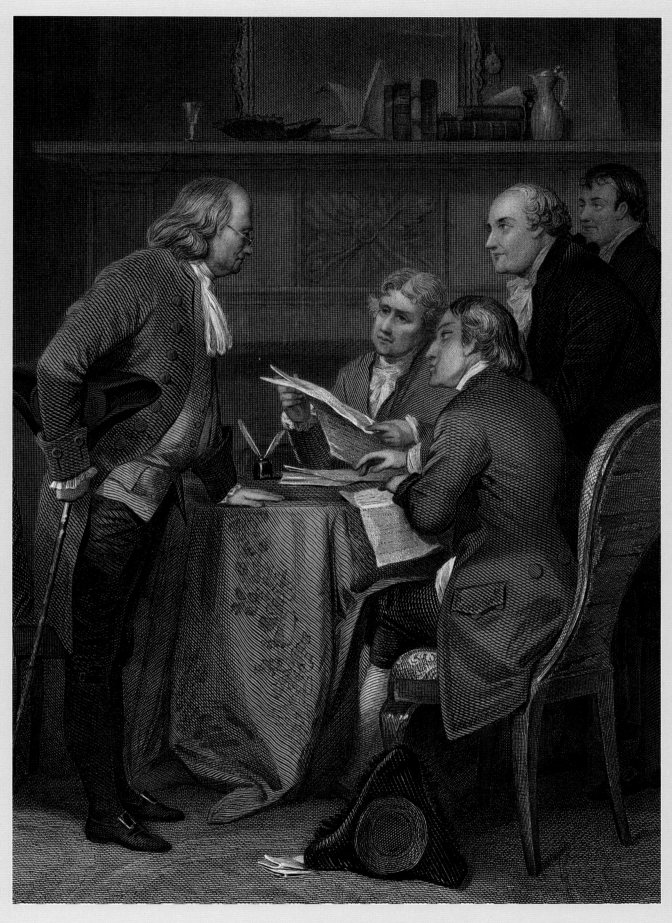

Two of the five men who drafted the Declaration of Independence – Benjamin Franklin (left) and Robert Livingston (second right) – were Freemasons, and another, Roger Sherman (far right), is thought to have been

British, they had no representation in the British parliament. Their slogan, 'No taxation without representation,' hit home with men (and women) throughout the colony. The smell of revolution was in the air.

In April 1775, a few months after a group of powerful colonists had met at the first Continental Congress and formed a Continental Association to enforce a boycott of British goods, the British commander-in-chief in North America, General Grace, sent troops from Boston to attack colonists in Lexington and Concord who, he had been warned, were preparing for armed insurgency.

The American War of Independence was under way.

In 1776, the [second] Continental Congress met in Philadelphia like the first. With colonists now in control of the city, they met at the old State House, the building that is now Independence Hall, and issued the Declaration of Independence. As most of the members of the Congress were influential landowners,

The Boston Tea Party, the night in 1773 when over 300 chests of English tea were thrown into the harbour by disgruntled Bostonians

merchants or successful businessmen – exactly the type of men who were attracted to Freemasonry – many of the men who attended were members of lodges in the areas they represented.

As with any issue that was certain to have far-reaching effects, there were Freemasons who opposed the Declaration and Freemasons who were for it. There is a widespread belief that many of its signatories were members of The Craft. In fact, out of the 56 men who penned their names to the famous document whose ringing words continue to strike a cord in the hearts of free-minded men the world over, only eight are definitely known to have been lodge members. And of the signatories to the subsequent Constitution of 1789, less than a quarter of them were Masons, although several were later initiated.

The Declaration was inspired by the writing of the English revolutionary Tom Paine, whose pamphlet *Common Sense* had urged the colonists to rebel against the rule of George III and declare the colony an independent republic. It has been claimed that Paine was a Freemason. Whilst this is not, in fact, true he was interested in it; indeed he wrote a treatise about it in which he traced the origins of The Craft, incorrectly, back to Welsh Druids.

The first man to sign the Declaration was John Hancock, who was a member of St Andrew's Lodge in Boston. He wrote his name extra-large and when asked why, he said it was so that King George could read it without having to put on his spectacles.

Other names forever linked with the Declaration and War of Independence who were Freemasons include John Paul Jones, the Scots-born founder of the US Navy, Richard Caswel, Mordecai Gist, James Jackson, Morgan Lewis and John Sullivan, all of whom became Grand Masters of their State Grand Lodges, and three of whom went on to serve as governors of their respective states.

And one of the most romantic names in US history, Paul Revere, who rode from Charleston to Lexington, rousing the militiamen in every town and village he rode through, to warn them that 'the British are coming' was an enthusiastic Freemason. He was entered into Boston's St Andrew's Lodge in 1760, when he was 25 and eventually became one of the Grand Masters of Massachusetts.

By 1781, the British realized that they were fighting a lost cause and made their peace with the rebels. The opening up of the United States was about to begin. In 1803, in what is known as the Louisiana Purchase, President Thomas Jefferson bought land from the French: not the present-day state of Louisiana, but all the land from the Mississippi–Missouri to the west coast. It wasn't long before settlers began to move from the eastern seaboard states into the vast new US territory, to farm, raise sheep and cattle and look for gold. Naturally, among the men who headed west were many Masons.

Now, far from their Mother Lodges, it was only natural that they started to form new lodges where they could meet in fellowship and practise The Craft. And it wasn't just new lodges they founded. Keen to be in charge of their own affairs, with some degree of independence from Washington, they founded territories with some degree of self-government, and these territories later became states with a much greater degree of autonomy

One by one, as each state or territory was founded, so a Grand Lodge for each one eventually came into being, authorizing new lodges within its area of jurisdiction. The first of the post-war Grand Lodges to be formed was in Maryland, where the first recorded lodge had been formed in 1750, warranted by the Grand Lodge of England and the St John's Pennsylvania Grand Lodge. The Maryland Grand Lodge was founded in 1783.

The most recent is Hawaii. Lodges there were originally warranted by the Grand Lodge of California, the Supreme Council of France and the Grand Lodge of Scotland through the then District Grand Lodge of Queensland, Australia. Eventually Hawaiian lodges came under the jurisdiction of California, which continued after the islands were granted statehood in 1959. It was not until 1989 that the twelve Hawaiian Lodges met in convention at the Honolulu Scottish Rite Cathedral and

constituted the Most Worshipful Grand Lodge of Free and Accepted Masons of the State of Hawaii.

As early as 1778, an attempt was made to establish a Grand Lodge for the entire United States, with George Washington as Grand Master, but this came to nothing and subsequent talk of such a Grand Lodge has met a similar fate. And so, today, there is a Grand Lodge for each state of the Union, fifty in all, plus another that governs the lodges that exist in the capital, Washington DC.

THE CAPITAL AND THE CAPITOL

Rather than site the new capital city in any of the then existing states, the founding fathers decided to build it in a specially designated area beyond the borders of any one state, thus avoiding any inter-state rivalry. The land on which the capital was built was ceded to Congress by Maryland in 1788 and Virginia in 1789, both states donating around 10 square miles for the purpose.

At the signing of the Declaration of Independence in 1776, eight of the signatories were Freemasons and another ten probably were

The influence of Freemasonry is, according to some authorities, very evident in the layout of the capital. One expert who believed that the plan was inspired by the instruments used in Freemasons' ritual wrote, 'Take any good street in downtown Washington DC and find the Capitol Building. Facing the Capitol from the Mall and using the Capitol building as the head or top of the Compass, the left leg is represented by Pennsylvania Avenue and the right leg, Maryland Avenue.' The left leg of the Compass, he believes, stands on the White House and the right leg on the Jefferson Memorial. 'The Square,' he writes, ' . . . is found in the usual Masonic position with the intersection of Canal Street and Louisiana Avenue.'

True or not, what is certain is that Freemasons were at the forefront of designing the new city and the Capitol Building itself was the creation of a succession of architects who were all members of The Craft. The original design is the work of William Thornton, completed by Benjamin Latrobe, who redesigned it after it was destroyed in 1814. The wings that flank the central building are the work of Thomas Walter.

The cornerstone of the original building was laid in 1793 with full Masonic honours under the auspices of the Grand Lodge of Maryland. George Washington, wearing his apron and full Masonic regalia, presided over the ceremony.

The influence of Freemasonry in the founding of the United States can also be seen on the back of a dollar bill. One of the first decisions made after the Declaration of Independence was to commission a Grand Seal. The design that was eventually chosen contains within it several Masonic symbols. The Great Seal itself is incorporated into the design of the dollar bill.

Washington was not just the first President of the United States, he was also the first in a long line of Freemasons to hold the office. They include James Monroe, who held office from 1817 to 1825, Andrew Jackson (1828–37), James Knox Polk (1845–49) and at least eleven more. The great Franklin Delano Roosevelt was entered on 11 October 1911, passed on 14 November and raised two weeks later in Holland Lodge No. 8, New York City. His successor in office, Harry S Truman was initiated in Missouri in 1909. A lifelong Freemason, he served as Grand Master of the Grand Lodge of Missouri, as well as being a Knight Templar and a 33° in the Scottish Rite.

Physical evidence of Freemasonry in the United States can be seen in the grand Masonic Temples that have been built, from Dallas in the south to Chicago in the north (the Temple there was the highest building in the city when it was built in 1892). But perhaps the best-known of all Masonic-inspired monuments, not just in the United States but anywhere in the world, stands on an island just off New York City – the Statue of Liberty.

A CENTENARY GIFT

During the American War of Independence, France, England's greatest imperial rival, sided with the Patriots, and during the French Revolutionary and Napoleonic Wars, the newly independent United States returned the compliment. As a mark of the historic friendship between the two countries, France decided to mark the centenary of the American Revolution by giving their US friends a memorial of some sort.

The idea for what was eventually built came to French architect and designer, Fredric Bartholdi, who was initiated into Freemasonry in 1874, as the ship in which he was sailing to America steamed into New York. As he gazed from the deck towards the land, he had a vision of a woman standing on a pedestal, holding aloft a torch in one hand as a beacon of welcome to immigrants coming to the New World in search of a new life.

Properly called 'Liberty Enlightening the World', the Statue of Liberty has welcomed millions of emigrants from other countries to the United States (many of whom were, no doubt, lodge members in their own lands and joined lodges in their new home).

Much of the money for the project was raised by Freemasons in France and in America, and when the cornerstone of the pedestal was laid in 1884, the Grand

Master of New York asked the assembled dignitaries why Freemasons had become so involved in the project. A few moments after he posed the question, he answered it himself: 'It's because no other organisation has ever done more to promote Liberty and to liberate men from their chains of ignorance and tyranny than Freemasonry.' Appropriately, when the statue was formally dedicated in 1886, thousands of Freemasons marched in procession through New York City.

One hundred years to the day after the cornerstone had been laid, a group of several thousand Freemasons gathered at the statue to commemorate the earlier

George Washington, first president of the United States, in full Masonic regalia at a lodge meeting where the laying of the cornerstone of the Capitol Building was discussed

ceremony and to rededicate themselves to what it stood for – freedom and liberty. The statue was in need of repair and a centenary restoration appeal had been launched. The gathered Freemasons pledged to raise money for the appeal. Every Grand Lodge in the United States contributed, and by the time the appeal closed they had raised two million dollars, one of the most substantial charitable donations ever to be made by non-government bodies.

The millions of visitors who visit Liberty Island every year read the large plaque, complete with square and compasses, that commemorates Freemasonry's role in the building of one of the most famous structures in the world.

THE MORGAN AFFAIR

In every country where Freemasonry has a presence, there are those who view it with suspicion, which is probably caused by fear of the unknown secret oaths they swear at their ceremonies and the dreadful (allegorical) punishments threatened to anyone who reveals Masonic ceremonies.

The United States is no exception. And even today, more than 180 years after the event, people who are suspicious of The Craft still mention the case of William Morgan to back their anti-Masonic views.

William Morgan was born in Virginia in 1774. His schooldays behind him, he left home and headed north, living for a time in Canada, taking whatever jobs were offered him, before arriving in Batavia, a small town in Genesee County in upstate New York, in 1824. There is no record of his ever having been entered, but it is thought he lied his way into at least one lodge in Rochester and another in Batavia.

In 1826, he made it known that he had written a book in which he revealed secrets of The Craft, and had received a large advance for it from the publisher of a local newspaper, David C. Millar. Freemasons in the area responded by painting Morgan as an undesirable character against whom everybody should be on their guard. Members of lodges in the area, many of them successful businessmen and tradesmen, organized a boycott of Miller's paper and withdrew their advertisements from it.

According to what has now become folklore in upstate New York, a local Freemason organized a cold supper for fifty men at a small inn 6 miles north of Batavia and let it be known that after their meal the men present were going to make their way to the town to attack Miller's offices. When Miller heard of the plan, he announced that he and a group of his friends, all armed, intended to defend his premises.

When the Freemasons, in turn, heard that Miller was planning an armed reception, they cancelled their plans. But two nights later a smaller group crept into Batavia and set fire to Miller's premises, torching bales of straw they had previously soaked in paraffin. As Miller set about putting out the flames, the Freemasons then went to Morgan's house and arrested him for debt – on what or whose authority is not on record.

With Morgan safely in jail for the weekend, the men forced their way into his house to look for the manuscript. They failed to find it.

On the following Monday, Miller paid the debt and Morgan was released. Almost immediately afterwards, he was rearrested on a charge of stealing a collar and tie and taken to Canandaigua, 50 miles east of Batavia, where he was again imprisoned.

On 13 September, a man called Lotan Lawson, said to have been a lodge member, turned up at the jail claiming to be a friend of Morgan and offered to stand surety for him. Witnesses claim that when the two men met, Morgan was obviously suspicious of the other man. He refused to get into Lawson's carriage whereupon two other men named Cheesebro and Sawyer appeared and bundled him into the waiting coach. Some of the onlookers who witnessed the event claim that as the carriage sped out of town, cries of 'Murder' rang out from within.

The carriage eventually stopped at Fort Niagara where Morgan was incarcerated in an old powder magazine. He seems to have been held there for several days before being taken to a waiting boat and rowed across the River Niagara into

The Statue if Liberty, a gift from the people of France to the people of the United States. Freemasons were prominent in its design and construction

A depiction of the murder of William Morgan. Never a member of a lodge, he acquired knowledge of The Craft and threatened to publish what he knew

Canadian territory. Apparently some Canadians were waiting, but when they were asked to 'dispose' of Morgan, they refused and he was rowed across the river and taken back to his cell.

That was the last time anyone saw (or admitted to having seen) William Morgan.

When his disappearance was noted, enemies of The Craft claimed he had been kidnapped and murdered. The anti-Freemasonry feelings this engendered were fuelled when David Miller published Morgan's book, which became an instant bestseller. Protesting their innocence in the matter, but forced on to the defensive, the Freemasons claimed that the whole incident had been nothing more than a publicity stunt cooked up by Miller and Morgan to promote the book.

There is no doubt that Lawson, Cheesebro and Sawyer, Freemasons all, had been involved in Morgan's abduction and they were all eventually put on trial and sentenced to 2 years', 1 year's and 3 months' imprisonment respectively. Before this, Governor De Witt Clinton of New York, a Freemason himself and furious that the Masons of Genesee County had brought The Craft into disrepute, offered first 300 and then 2,000 dollars as a reward for information about Morgan's whereabouts.

Some time later a body was washed ashore 40 or so miles downstream from Fort Niagara. It was initially identified as being Morgan but it was later established beyond reasonable doubt that the body was not Morgan's but that of an unfortunate Canadian man who had fallen into the river and been swept away.

Morgan's body was never found. Some say that he escaped from his cell at the fort and, fearing for his life, became a hermit; others that he became a pirate and was hanged; and yet others that he ended his days on a Caribbean island, having been shipwrecked there in the last days of 1827.

Whatever the truth, what is beyond doubt is that the mystery surrounding the disappearance of William Morgan caused huge damage to Freemasonry in the United States. A wave of anti-Freemasonry feeling swept the country. Lodges were attacked by angry mobs and the contents destroyed: many were forced to close. Friendships were ruined and families split down the middle between those who believed that the Morgan case was evidence that the Freemasons were a nefarious group of kidnappers and murderers and those who held that The Craft had a worthwhile role to play in society.

Five years after the event, an anti-Freemasonry candidate ran for the presidency. He failed and the hysteria started to die down, but it was not until the middle of the century that Freemasonry started to shake itself free from the belief that its members were guilty as charged by public opinion. Even today, the name of William Morgan is still used by those who see Freemasonry as a force for evil, rather than the power for good that it is.

A QUESTION OF DEGREES

The United States has a rich diversity of Masonic and quasi-Masonic organizations each with its own lodges, rites and number of degrees to which members can aspire. And there can hardly be a town from the eastern seaboard to the Pacific coast and from the border with Canada in the north to the boundary with Mexico in the south in which Freemasonry has not established a presence.

There was, and still is, some resistance to The Craft from Mormons who at one time attempted to gain control of several lodges in Illinois. This resulted in animosity, which in some cases ran so deep that it persists to this day.

Freemasonry, as a multi-racial organisation, represents every race in US lodges including, naturally, Afro-Americans, many of whom follow Prince Hall Masonry. Hall was the first black American Freemason: a freeman and a Methodist minister, he was made a Mason in Cambridge, Massachusetts, in an Irish military lodge in 1775. A few years afterwards he wrote to the Grand Lodge of England, asking it to authorize him to establish a new lodge. The charter, for African Lodge No. 459, was duly issued (and still survives) but took 3 years to reach him. So it was not until 1791 that the African Grand Lodge was founded with Hall as Grand Master.

Unfortunately, there were irregularities in the lodge submitting reports and payments, and it was erased by England. Undaunted, Hall constituted on his own authority a further lodge at Providence, Rhode Island, which continued after his death in 1808. In 1827 it declared itself to be African Grand Lodge No. 1. As the years passed, more lodges were chartered and Prince Hall Grand Lodges began to appear in several states.

Today, although they remain outside the fold of regular US Grand Lodges, they

A French engraving from the eighteenth century depicting a reception for Master Masons

continue to attract members who are as devoted to the ideals and virtues of Freemasonry as their more conventional brothers.

Major among the rites followed is the Scottish Rite, more usually called the Ancient and Accepted (Scottish) Rite, a 33° system that evolved out of the eighteenth-century French Rite of Perfection. The latter rite was organized by one Stephen Morin in the West Indies in the early 1760s. Four or five years later it was taken to North America by his friend Henry Franklin, who established a Lodge of Perfection in Albany, the state capital of New York.

Franklin was succeeded by the Comte de Grasse-Tilly, who added five degrees to the Rite, giving it the present 33° structure. He was also influential in establishing the first Scottish Rite Supreme Council in the South Carolina city of Charleston, which was eventually formed in 1801 when the first Supreme Council was formed by Colonel John Mitchell. The elegant town house in which the Council in Charleston met was the forerunner of many arresting and elegant office buildings and temples associated with the Scottish Rite in the United States.

The early history of the Rite is one of confusion and chaos, especially in the northern states, where it was riven by rivalries and schisms and competing Supreme Councils. In the south it was dominated by one man, Albert Pike, who was elected Sovereign Grand Commander of the Supreme Council (Southern Jurisdiction) in 1859 and held office until his death in 1891. Under his leadership, the Rite expanded hugely, attracting then as it continues to do, Masons searching perhaps for a more spiritual and philosophical approach to The Craft than others.

After attaining Master Mason rank, those who wish to attain the 33rd degree, must achieve the following:

4th degree	Perfect Master
5th degree	Perfect Master
6th degree	Intimate Secretary
7th degree	Provost and Judge
8th degree	Intendant of the Building
9th degree	Master Elect of Nine
10th degree	Elect of Fifteen
11th degree	Sublime Master Elect
12th degree	Grand Master Architect
13th degree	Master of the Ninth Arch
14th degree	Grand Elect Mason
15th degree	Knight of the East of Sword
16th degree	Prince of Jerusalem
17th degree	Knight of the East and West
18th degree	Knight of the Rose Croix
19th degree	Grand Pontiff
20th degree	Master Ad Vitam
21st degree	Patriarch Noachite
22nd degree	Prince of Libanis
23rd degree	Chief of the Tabernacle
24th degree	Prince of the Tabernacle
25th degree	Knight of the Brazen Temple
26th degree	Prince of Mercy
27th degree	Commander of the Temple
28th degree	Knight of the Sun
29th degree	Knight of St Andrew
30th degree	Grand Elect Knight K-H
31st degree	Grand Inspector Inquisitor
32nd degree	Sublime Prince of the Royal Secret
33rd degree	Sovereign Grand Inspector General

Another major American Rite is the York Rite, which claims descent from the legendary Assembly of Masons summoned by Prince Edwin at York in AD 926 (see p. 31). Once they have been raised to Master Mason, those who wish to climb to the top step of the York Rite must advance a further seven stages which are known by name rather than degree number. The first such step is that of Mark Master, followed in turn by Past Master, Most Excellent Master, Royal Arch Mason (which itself has three degrees – Royal Master, Select Master and Super Excellent Master. The next steps are the Order of the Red Cross, the Order of Knights of Malta and at the top of the tree is the Order of Knight Templar.

Those who reach the ultimate stages in either the Scottish or York Rite are eligible for membership of the Ancient Order of Nobles of the Mystic Shrine. The 'Shriners' are known in the United States for their flamboyant parades, which see their members in fancy dress following marching bands to raise money for charity. Since the order was founded in the 1870s, its members have donated countless millions for good causes. Their dinners are also famed not just for the food on offer, but for the entertainment they provide, and are perhaps the only Masonic body to be mentioned in a hit Broadway show. In *Gypsy*, the Stephen Sondheim musical based on the life of Gypsy Rose Lee, when Mama is dreaming of her plans for the future, she sings 'Goodbye to blueberry pie. . . All the Shriners I said hello to'.

Other Masonic or quasi-Masonic bodies in the United States include the Order of DeMoley, the Grotto and the Tall Cedars of Lebanon, and, for women, the Rainbow Girls, Job's Daughters, the Order of the Eastern Star and the Daughters of the Nile (restricted to wives of Shriners).

THE ROYAL ARCH

In the English tradition, the Royal Arch is seen as the completion of the Master Mason degree. In 1813, the Mother Grand Lodge decreed:

'Pure, ancient Freemasonry consists of but three degrees: that of Entered Apprentice, Fellow Craft and Master Mason, including the Supreme Order of the Holy Royal Arch, members of which are known as Companions.'

Having learned all The Craft has to teach them about living a life of which 'God' will approve and of service to their fellow humankind, Companions are encouraged to find ways of improving their individual relationship with their God.

In other traditions, the Arch is a separate degree independent of The Craft but linked to it and drawing men who see the traditional three Degrees as but the first step in their Masonic education

Historians have traced its origins to Ireland in the late seventeenth century and in England to 1738. In the United States there are records that the Royal Arch Degree was conferred on members of the Fredericksburg Lodge No. 4 in December 1753, the lodge in which George Washington had been raised.

The Arch consists of four degrees; Mark Master, Past Master, Most Excellent Master and Royal Arch Mason. The Most Excellent Master Degree is an American innovation, conferred in a Royal Arch Chapter in 1783 in a lodge in Connecticut.

Fourteen years later, in 1797, the General Grand Chapter, Royal Arch Masons was founded in Boston, Massachusetts. It now has jurisdiction over many Chapters in the States, Central and South America, and several provinces in Canada.

THE CRAFT IN CANADA

To many people, the United States is North America, thus ignoring the vast country, the second largest in the world, that lies north of the 49th Parallel – Canada.

The first record of a lodge in Canada occurs in 1749, at Annopolis in Nova Scotia, and The Craft has had a presence in the country ever since. When the Seven Years War broke out in Europe in 1757, both Britain and France saw it as an opportunity to gain territory in the New World. French and English troops faced each other in Canada and during the war military lodges were established in Quebec.

Four years after the War came to an end in 1767, and with Canada firmly a British territory (although there were many French settlers), a Provincial Grand Lodge was established. Most of the early Canadian lodges followed the English tradition, but with a strong Scottish and Irish presence, both military and civilian, their respective Grand Lodges at home were asked to warrant military and stationary lodges in the province. And being so close to the American colony, at least one Canadian lodge was warranted by the Grand Lodge of New York.

When the American Revolution broke out, thousands of colonists loyal to the Crown packed their bags and headed north for Canada. Many of the Freemasons among them were instrumental in establishing the Provincial Grand Lodges of Upper and Lower Canada. In 1858, the first Grand Lodge of Canada was established, many members of the lodges it warranted being descendants of those British loyalists.

1858 was significant in Canadian history as the year that gold was discovered in the west, in British Columbia. Many of the men who headed for the gold fields to seek their fortune, and those who followed in their wake, were members of lodges back in the east, and they took The Craft with them. They established lodges that were loyal to both the English and Scottish traditions, depending on their particular allegiance.

It wasn't long after the province was granted dominion status in 1867 that Grand

Lodges were constituted for all nine provinces. Newfoundland remained outside the dominion until after the Second World War, and even after it joined it retained its Masonic ties with the United Kingdom.

Today, Freemasonry flourishes in Canada, along with the Royal Arch and the additional degrees found in the United States, some of which are controlled by independent Canadian bodies, some governed from the United States.

As with its cousin south of the border, Freemasons have played a vital part in the civic and political life of the country, and six of Canada's prime ministers have been active in The Craft.

When gold was found in a previously undeveloped part of Canada, Freemasons were among the prospectors. These men took their Craft with them, and so Freemasonry spread across the country

The Supreme Royal Arch Chapter in Edinburgh. The pillars and ornate ceiling seen here are a common theme throughout Freemasonry

RITES AND RITUALS

Rites and rituals vary from order to order, from degree to degree, but when a prospective Mason is entered, an Entered Apprentice passed in the Fellow Craft degree and the Fellow Craft raised to Master Mason, the ceremonies of all have much in common. And the roles of the officers of the Lodge are common to most orders. . .

After the Articles of Union were agreed and subsequently signed in 1813, a Lodge of Reconciliation was warranted to establish uniformity in matters of ritual. However, the steadfast refusal to allow rituals to be printed, in an effort to protect the secrecy of the proceedings, meant that there was a wide variety in the way in which rituals proceeded within the lodges. Nevertheless there are certain elements that almost all Freemasonic degrees have in common.

The candidate, be it for Apprenticeship, Fellow Craft or Mastery, has to undergo careful preparation. He is dressed symbolically and spends time to prepare himself mentally and physically for the rituals to follow.

The rituals involve taking a symbolic pilgrimage that leads to a spiritual goal that is not made known in one single revelation, but gradually. During this journey the candidate has to undergo symbolic trials and dangers that test his commitment and courage, his integrity and trustworthiness.

It is usual for part of the journey to take place in the dark, which may be either actual or figurative, and for it to finish in a startling restoration of the light. This is representative of the move from spiritual and moral ignorance, or darkness, into the light of understanding and knowledge.

The journey over, the move from darkness to light is confirmed by the candidate, now accepted or raised, being symbolically robed and clad in regalia. As this is being done, the symbolic meaning of each item is explained to him.

THE LODGE

Before looking at the ceremonies involved in being initiated and progressing from degree to degree, we will look at the Lodge itself, for it is much more than the Masonic meeting place. Everything in it has a symbolic meaning, as indeed does the Lodge itself.

The Lodge is supported by the three pillars of Wisdom, Strength and Beauty, its floor a chequer-board of black and white squares that denote the duality of terrestrial life: the pleasures of one are the pain of others; what one may see as positive, another may regard as negative.

And if the floor represents man's earthy nature, the ceiling – 'a symbolic celestial canopy of divers colours' – represents the ethereal.

The Lodge is illuminated, figuratively speaking, by the Three Great and the Three Lesser Lights. The Great Lights are unlimited by time and space, while the the Three Lesser ones are limited by both.

The Great Lights – the Holy Book, the square and the compass – are the symbols most commonly associated with Freemasonry. The Book rules the Mason's faith, the square governs his actions and the compasses create a bond with all mankind, but especially with fellow Masons.

The Lesser Lights light the Mason to, at and from his labour. They are situated in

the east, west and south, an allusion to the course of the sun, which rises in the east, reaches its meridian in the south and disappears in the west. The Sun, the Moon and the Master of the Lodge are emblematic of the Three Lesser Lights.

Officially the Lodge is 'an oblong square; in length between East and West and in breadth between North and South, in depth from the surface of the earth to its centre, and even as high as the heavens'.

Many authorities take this slightly arcane definition as alluding not just to the physical room, but to the Mason himself. Just as a Masonic Lodge is a meeting of brethren and fellows 'met to expiate upon the mysteries of The Craft' so the individual Mason is made up of various properties and faculties. These are assembled within him and interact harmoniously in such a way as to enable the individual to work out the purpose of his own life.

Every Mason is, in effect, his own Lodge. So, when a man expresses a desire to begin his journey into The Craft and to be entered in the First Degree as an Apprentice, he is taking the first step on the long journey of getting to know himself.

Freemasonry is not alone in holding what some may call a conceit. When a youngster is confirmed into the Christian faith, he or she is taking the same first step; so, too, is the young man or women who decides to follow the Buddha. The difference between these faiths and Freemasonry is of course that Freemasonry is not a religion or a faith (indeed, discussion on any such topic within the Lodge is not allowed).

The four sides of the Lodge remind the Mason of the ancient belief that the human body is composed of four elements, which exist in balanced proportions in the rarely achieved perfect state. Water represents our physical nature; Air is symbolic of our mentality; Fire of the will and nervous energy we all have to some degree or other, and it is in Earth that the other three become encased and stabilized.

But we have a spiritual side to our nature as well as a physical one. The oblong-shaped Lodge represents them both.

It is not just the shape of the Lodge that has a symbolic meaning. Each side of the Lodge has its own significance, too.

The East is representative of man's spirituality, which in most of us is hardly developed, if at all. But it is there, and in making the Masonic Journey from Apprentice to Fellow Craft, from Fellow Craft to Master Mason, from there to the Royal Arch and, in several rites beyond, that the Mason is making a conscious effort to develop this spirituality.

Just as West lies opposite East, so its symbolic meaning is opposite. West represents our normal, rational understanding of things. If East is spiritual, then West is common sense.

The two come together in the South, the meeting place of spiritual intuition and rationality and symbol of the point where abstract intellectuality and intellectual power fuse and complement one another in perfect balance.

And just as West and East have their opposite symbolic meaning, so North is opposite to South. It is the meridian of ignorance, the point of instinctive, usually wrong, reaction to events. It is the lowest common denominator of our being.

So, the four sides of the Lodge combine to make up the four possible ways in which we acquire knowledge. North is self-impression; West is reason; South is the intellect and East is spiritual intuition. Of the four, most of us use only the first two in our development and education, and so our outlook on life and our regard for truth are restricted and therefore imperfect.

There are some of us who nod in South's direction as we go through our daily lives. But perfect and full knowledge of ourselves and the world in which we must function is only conscious when our spiritual selves have been awakened and we consciously acknowledge it in our every thought, word and deed.

In Masonic terms, it is only the Master who has completed his journey who has at his disposal all four methods of acquiring knowledge in perfect balance and adjustment, just as the four sides of the Lodge are in perfect harmony.

*A membership certificate of the United Grand Lodge of England. The certificate is dominated by the
Three Pillars – Wisdom, Strength and Beauty – which must be present in every lodge. Wisdom constructs the building,
Beauty adorns it and Strength supports it*

THE LODGE'S OFFICERS

There are six other officers of the Lodge, making a total of seven, a number which is regarded as athat of 'universal completeness'. The seven days of the Creation, the seven colours of the spectrum, the seven ages of man . . . the number is significant even in the realm of folklore and superstition. To be the seventh son of a seventh son (or seventh daughter of a seventh daughter) is to be bestowed with the gift of prophesy.

But back to the Lodge . . . as well as having their own functions in Lodge proceedings, each of the offices is connected symbolically to a part of the human mechanism.

As we have seen, the most senior of the seven is the Worshipful Master, in military terms the commanding officer in charge of the Lodge. He represents the spiritual in Man. Just as when the Supreme Being speaks to us in ourselves, our response should always be immediate and sympathetic; so when the Worshipful Master acts, the Lodge responds. When his gavel knocks, others in the Lodge repeat the knock. He represents what has been called the Divine Principle in us. Without this, we would be sub-human; with it we become more than human. And so, in the Lodge, it is the Worshipful Master's presence that gives the its activities their authority. In the words of one of The Craft's historians, 'It is the inextinguishable light of a Master Mason, which, being immortal and eternal, continues to shine when everything temporal and mortal has disappeared.'

Continuing the military analogy, the Senior Warden is the second-in-command, but symbolically he is his senior officer's opposite. For whereas the Master represents the spiritual, the Senior Warden is the personification of the soul, and is associated with the psychic aspect of humankind, something which, if it has no association with the greater light of the spirit, has no light of its own. Just as our moon depends on the sun for the light it transmits to the earth, so the Senior Warden, positioned in the West, depends on his authority coming from the Master in the East, and which he passes on to the others in the Lodge.

In the South is the Junior Warden, personifying the point between the spiritual and the psyche where these two meet in perfect balance and interact harmoniously. The Mason who has advanced to the Second Degree has realized that the Supreme Being is not outside him, but is part of him. This enlightenment can only come with the struggle to try to overcome one's own imperfections and limitations. Representing enlightenment as he does, it is the Junior Warden who asserts in the ceremony of the Second Degree when the Apprentice advances to Fellow Craft that he has been enabled in that degree:

Worshipful Master:	Brother Junior Warden are you a Fellow Craft Freemason?
Junior Warden:	I am: try me: prove me.
Worshipful Master:	By what instrument of architecture will you be proved?
Junior Warden:	By the square.
Worshipful Master:	What is the square?
Junior Warden:	An angle of ninety degrees, forming the fourth part of a circle.

Having been entered as Apprentice, a newly-elected member of a French Lodge swears the Oath on The Book. The cloth around which other members of the Lodge stand, bears the symbols appropriate to the rank

The Senior Deacon is the Master's adjutant and emissary, forming a link between East and West. The Junior Deacon fulfils the same function for the Senior Warden and creates a link between West and South.

The Inner Guard is under the immediate control of the Junior Warden and acts in what has been described in mutually reflex action with the Outer Guard or contact point with the outer-world.

At the risk of causing mirth to those who see Freemasonry as little more than a you-scratch-my-back-and-I'll-scratch-your-back organization and Masonic meetings as a good excuse for a good dinner, the symbolic meaning ascribed to the various offices can be summed up thus:

Worshipful Master	The Spirit
Senior Warden	The Soul
Junior Warden	The Intellect
The Senior Deacon	The link between the Spirit and the Soul
The Junior Deacon	The link between the Soul and the Mind
The Inner Guard	The inner self
The Outer Guard	The outer self

An Apprentice is entered into a French lodge in the mid-nineteenth century. Traditionally such ceremonies are held in semi-darkness and the words of the ritual are committed to memory, never to paper

THE LODGE MEETING

Presiding over a Lodge meeting is the Master, who is often styled Worshipful Master. Past Masters, who, as the title suggests, are men who have served as Master, are also usually present. As we have just seen, immediately beneath the Master is the Senior Warden, then the Junior Warden, Senior and Junior Deacons and lastly an Inner Guard and Tylers, or doorkeepers, one inside, the other outside, who are often armed with a ceremonial sword.

When the Lodge members are assembled, the Master brings it to order with a knock (or series of knocks, depending on the purpose of the Lodge), which is then repeated by the Warden.

There then follows a dialogue between the Master and one of the Wardens, during which the senior man directs that the Lodge be properly tiled and that the

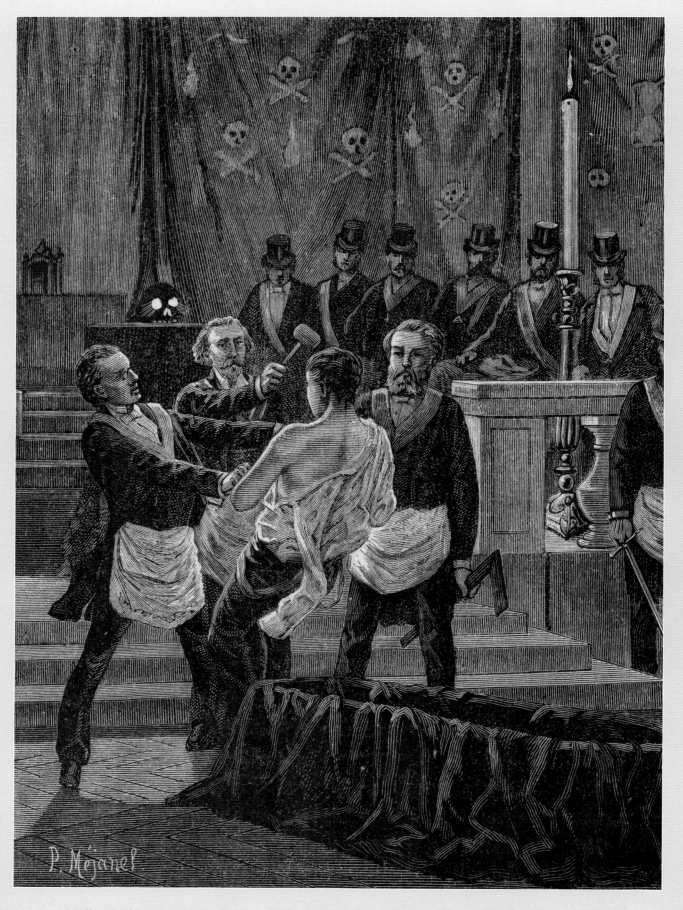

A Fellow Craft is raised to Master in a French Lodge. This action represents the 'death of Self' and the candidate's willingness to surrender it to the Deity. Only one who has taken responsibility for his own life in this way is entitled to 'demand admission' to the Master Mason's degree

various duties are done. He asks, for example where the Tylers are placed and what their respective duties are.

When the Master is satisfied that everything is in order and that all the officers are in their proper places and aware of their respective duties, he declares the Lodge duly formed. Before proceeding to declare it open, he invokes a blessing from the Great Architect of the Universe, asking that the Lodge having been begun in order, may be conducted in peace and closed in harmony.

That done, a series of knocks announces that the Lodge is opened. The assembled brethren take their seats and the business of the Lodge begins. If there is any doubt about the right of any of those present to be there, they are asked to vow that they are proper Masons and that they have not been expelled by any lodge.

It is at the appropriate Lodge meetings that newcomers to The Craft are initiated into it as Apprentices, Apprentices passed to Fellow Craft and Fellow Craft to Master.

The practices described herewith may have changed since they were being practised by one lodge in the nineteenth century, but the underlying philosophy behind them is common throughout lodges the world over.

THE CEREMONY OF THE FIRST DEGREE

A candidate who has applied to be initiated in the First or Entered Apprentice's Degree has, figuratively speaking, asked to be admitted to the ground floor of King Solomon's Temple. He has to sign a declaration that he wishes to be a Mason. When this has been presented to the Lodge and approved, usually by ballot of the brethren.

At the ceremony one of the brethren, often the Steward, is sent into the antechamber in which the candidate is waiting. According to one nineteenth-century authority, Richard Carlile:

> *This preparation consists in the candidate being divested of all money and metal, of having his right arm, left breast and left knee bare, the right heel slip-shod: in then being blindfolded and a rope, which is technically called a Cable Tow is put round the neck with a sword pointed to the breast. In this state, the Steward leads the candidate to the Tyler or Outer Guard of the Lodge Door. The Tyler examines him and, on seeing the candidate properly prepared, he announces his approach by three knocks.*

All Freemasons vow during their initiation never to 'reveal any part or parts, point or points, of the secrets and mysteries of, or belonging to, free and accepted masons which have been, shall now or hereafter be communicated to me'.

The penalty for anyone breaking this vow is the sort of thing of which nightmares are made: '. . . to have my throat cut across, my tongue torn out by the root, and my body buried in the sand of the sea at low water mark, or a cable's length from the shore where the tide regularly ebbs and flows twice in twenty-four hours.' Or he may simply be branded as a perjurer, devoid of all moral worth and unfit to be received in any other warranted lodge. (Of the two, one knows which of these one would prefer!)

THE TOOLS OF THE FIRST DEGREE

The oath administered, the ceremony proceeds, the various signs and secrets of the Entered Apprentice (the handgrip and the password 'Boaz!') are revealed and the prescribed tools – the 24-inch gauge, the gavel and the chisel – presented. The Master explains the practical worth of each.

The gauge is the first instrument put into the hands of a workman, enabling him to measure and ascertain the size and extent of the work to be engaged in and so to calculate the time and labour it will need.

The gavel, he tells the Apprentice, is recognized by various artists and called different names by different groups. But all of them admit that no manual work can be completed without it.

The sharpness of the chisel compensates for its size, and allows it to make an impression on the hardest substance.

But it is what each tool symbolizes that is more important to the speculative Mason. The gauge with its twenty-four divisions represents the hours of the day and directs the Apprentice to apportion them properly to prayer, labour, refreshment and sleep.

The gavel teaches that skill without exertion is of no use: man was born to labour – the heart conceives and the head devises in vain if the hand is not prompt to execute the design.

The lesson of the chisel is that perseverance is necessary to establish perfection.

Together, the three tell the Apprentice that 'knowledge grounded on accuracy, aided by labour, prompted by perseverance, will finally overcome all difficulties, raise ignorance from despair, and establish happiness in paths of science'.

The Master then congratulates the Apprentice on being admitted to the ancient and honourable craft of Freemasonry and charges him in his various duties and responsibilities he owes God, his neighbours and himself. He advises the new Freemason to let prudence direct his actions, to be temperate, to let justice be the guide to all actions and expresses the hope that he will supported by fortitude. The necessity for secrecy, fidelity and obedience are also stressed.

The meeting then proceeds to a lecture on the First Degree Tracing Board.

In the days of operative masonry, these boards, also called trestle boards, were the boards on which the architect or builder traced out the ground plan of the building to be constructed. In adoptive Freemasonry, they offer a pictorial, symbolic depiction of the principles associated with a particular degree.

In his book, *Freemasonry, a Journey through Ritual and Symbol*, W. Kirk Mcnulty (Thames & Hudson, London, 1991) offers a fascinating guide to tracing board symbolism. The items included in each one have not just a symbolic meaning, but a deeply psychological one as well.

The First Degree board, with its chequered floor and soaring pillars, its depiction of Jacob's Ladder, its blazing centre and glowing sun, represents the individual and his place in the universe. The Tracing Board of the Second Degree shows Jacob's Ladder as the staircase that the Freemason must climb in his spiritual journey, turning away from the physical world to concentrate instead on his spiritual existence. The Third Degree board tries to capture the idea that it is only through death that an individual can fully realize the potential that life offers.

The compass and the square, perhaps the tools most commonly associated in most people's minds with Freemasonry. Along with the Book, they constitute the Three Great Lights or the Furniture of the Lodge

FROM APPRENTICE TO FELLOW CRAFT

When a candidate is to be passed to the Second Degree, a Lodge of the First Degree is opened (at which all present apart from the one to be passed are themselves at least of Fellow Craft rank). The candidate to be passed is then asked where he was first prepared to be a Freemason (the correct answer to which is 'In my heart') and then posed several more prescribed questions to which there are prescribed answers.

The would-be Fellow Craft is then asked to pledge that he will keep secret the passing grip and password leading to the door of the Lodge into which he seeks to be admitted. The pledge given, the information is passed and the candidate led from the room.

The Lodge is now opened in the Second Degree. To do so, the Master Warden directs that the Lodge be properly tiled. That done, he asks the Junior Warden what the next 'care' is to be. On hearing that it is to 'see the Brethren appear as Fellow-Craft Masons', he asks the junior officer first that he is a Fellow-Craft and then 'by what instrument he will be proved'. Once satisfied that the Junior Warden is himself of the Second Degree, the Master directs him to prove that all those present be Fellow-Craft Masons by threefold signs.

Happy that everyone in the Lodge has been passed in the Second Degree, the Warden declares the Lodge formed, but before opening it he invokes a blessing from the Great Geometrician or Architect of the Universe. He now declares the Lodge open on the Square (the first of the Second Degree working tools, and the one on which the Junior Warden proved his Fellow Craft) for the instruction and improvement of Fellow Craft Freemasons.

The proper knocks are then given and the assembled group take their seats. Meanwhile, in the antechamber, the Tyler questions the candidate regarding the passing grip and word. The door is then knocked on and the Inner Guard demands to know who is there. He, the Inner Guard, then reports to the Master that there is, at the door of the Lodge, a brother who has been properly initiated and has made

The ladder leading to Heaven, which, according to Genesis 28, Jacob dreamed of as he lay asleep. It symbolizes the journey that the individual must make in turning his thoughts away from things physical to matters spiritual

such progress as he hopes will recommend him to be passed to the degree of Fellow Craft. He also assures the Master that the candidate comes properly prepared.

According to Richard Carlile, the authority previously quoted, the ceremony proceeds and sees the candidate hooded and with left arm, right breast and right knee made bare and left heel slipshod. After being led three times round the Lodge, he is asked to kneel in a particular fashion based on the square and the compasses and to swear the oath of secrecy. The penalty for breaking it is particularly savage, involving those promised to a wayward Apprentice, with the added threat of having the left breast cut open, the heart torn out and given to 'ravenous birds of the air' or 'the devouring beasts of the field as a prey'.

The oath administered and taken, the Master bids the candidate to rise as a Fellow Craft Freemason and imparts the grip of the Fellow Craft and the passing word, 'Jachin'. In doing so, he makes several allusions to King Solomon and his Temple.

The tools of the Fellow Craft are then presented – the square, the level and the plumb-rule. The square, used by masons to try and adjust all irregular corners of a building and to assist 'in bringing rude matters into due form' symbolizes morality. The level, which proves horizontals, signifies equality. And the plumb-rule to adjust all uprights equates to justice and uprightness in life.

The Charges of the Second Degree are then read and the new Fellow Craft exhorted to 'persevere in the practice of virtue'. In a hark to past, it is also recommended that he study the liberal arts, particularly 'the science of geometry and masonry'. He is encouraged to contribute to discussions and offer his opinions freely, while respecting the opinions of others. The necessity of support not just fellow Freemasons who are in need, but all his fellow human kind.

After a lecture on the tracing board of the Second Degree and any other business, the lodge is brought to an end with due ceremony, the Master commanding the Senior Warden to bring proceedings to a conclusion. He does so in the name of Grand Geometrician of the Universe and by command of the Worshipful Master.

THE THIRD OR MASTER MASON'S DEGREE

The Third Degree, that of being raised from Fellow Craft to Master Mason, is the final one in the English Tradition. Thereafter, the Master Mason may proceed to the Royal Arch, which completes the journey by symbolically rebuilding the Temple. In other traditions and rites, the Master Mason can proceed to many more degrees, thirty-three in the case of the Ancient and Accepted Scottish Rite, which is widely practised in the United States.

The ceremony of the Third Degree is associated with the death of Hiram, the man who built King Solomon's Temple. The figurative raising from the dead that is part of the ritual is not representative of a resurrection as Christ's is for Christians, but represents the loss of hope and its eventual restoration.

Just as in the Fellow Craft ritual described above, a First Degree Lodge was opened at the start of proceedings; at a meeting where a Fellow Craft is to be raised

to Master or to the Third Degree, a Lodge of the Second Degree is first opened.

The candidate is asked a series of questions on his qualification as Fellow Craft and, on pledging that he will reveal them to no man, is given the information leading to the degree into which he is to be admitted. He is then led from the Lodge to be properly prepared for the ritual to come. Both his arms, breast and knees are bared and both heels slip-shod.

While this is being done, the Master opens a Lodge of the Third Degree in much the same way as lodges of lower degrees are readied.

After the candidate has been introduced, entered the Lodge, been shown the grip and has been told the password, 'Tubal Cain' (he is later given the secret word of the Master Mason, which is 'Machaben', 'Machbinna' or 'Mahabone'). He then kneels before the Master of the Lodge who asks the Supreme Being to strengthen the candidate for the ordeal to come.

He is then led three times round the room, showing the signs and grips of the Apprentice and Fellow Craft to the Lodge officials. Then, after making a very long and very solemn pledge during which he vows, should he err, to have his body cut in two, his bowels torn out, his remains burned to ashes and scattered north, south,

Part of the ritual during which a lodge member is raised to the Master Mason's degree

113

east and west so that no trace of him is left among men, he is subject to a very long and solemn 'ordeal'. During this the candidate is symbolically struck on the forehead and forced to feign the death of Hiram Abiff (see p. 11). The Fellow Craft is then duly raised to Master Mason and the secrets of the rank revealed to him.

Now he is presented with a skirret, pencil and compasses. The first points to the straight and undeviating line of conduct laid down in sacred law, and the second serves as a reminder that all words and actions are recorded by the Supreme Being, who must be accounted to at life's end. The compasses stand for that being's unerring and impartial justice.

The ritual is brought to an end with the new Master Mason answering another series of questions, which in one Lodge used to run as follows. The slightly archaic flavour of the language lends a suitable sincerity to the ritual of question of answer.

How were you prepared to be made a Master Mason?
Both my arms, both breasts, both knees made bare and both heels slip-shod.

On what did you enter?
Upon both points of the compasses presented to both my breasts.

On your entrance to the lodge did you observe anything different from its usual appearance?
I did: all was dark, save one glimmering light in the east.

To what did the darkness allude?
Even to the darkness of death.

Am I given to understand that death is the peculiar subject of the degree?
You are.

From what circumstance?
From the untimely death of Master Hiram Abiff.

What were the instruments made use of at his destruction?
The plumb-rule, level and heavy maul.

How came you in possession of those secrets?
From having figuratively represented him when I was raised to the sublime Degree of Master Mason.

How were you raised?
Upon the five points of Fellowship.

Which I will thank you to name and afterwards explain.
First, hand to hand; second, foot to foot; third, knee to knee; fourth, breast to breast; and fifth, hand over back.

First, hand to hand. I greet you as a brother, and when the necessities of a brother call for my aid and support, I will be ever ready to hand him such assistance to save him from sinking, if I find him worthy thereof, as may not be detrimental to myself of connections.

Second, foot to foot. I will support you in all just and laudable undertakings. Indolence shall not cause my footsteps to halt, nor wrath to turn them aside. But forgetting every selfish consideration, I will ever be swift of foot to save, help and to execute benevolence to a fellow creature in distress, but more particularly to a Brother Mason, if worthy.

Third, knee to knee, being the posture of my daily supplication, shall remind me of your wants. When I offer up my ejaculations to Almighty God, a brother's welfare I will remember as my own; for, as the voices of the babes

Having been raised to the Third Degree, a new Master Mason kneels before the Master of the Lodge

and sucklings ascend to the throne of grace so most assuredly will the breathings of a fervent heart ascend to the mansion of bliss, as our prayers are certainly received for each other.

Fourth, breast to breast, that my breast shall be a safe and sacred repository for all your just and lawful secrets. A brother's secrets delivered to me as such, I would keep as my own, as to betray that trust might be doing him the greatest injury he could sustain in his mortal life; nay it would be like the villainy of an assassin, who lurks in the darkness to stab his adversary, when unarmed and least prepared to meet an enemy.

Fifth, hand over back, that I will support a brother's character in his absence, equally as though he were present. I will not wrongly revile him myself, nor will I suffer it to be done by others if my power to prevent it.

Thus, by the five points of fellowship, are we linked together in one indivisible chain of sincere affection, brotherly love, relief and truth.

The new Master duly raised, and any other business dealt with, the Master directs that the Lodge be 'close tiled'. After due ritual the Master of the Lodge tells the Senior Warden in words reminiscent of Shakespeare that 'our labours now are ended' in this degree and that he, the Senior Warden has the Master's command to close the Master Mason's Lodge.

The Senior Warden advises the brethren that by the command of the Master the Master Mason's Lodge is declared closed. His words are echoed by the Junior Warden that it is 'accordingly closed, and with final knocks from him, the Inner Guard and the Tyler, the Lodge is ended.

THE HOLY ROYAL ARCH

Roughly a third of English Master Masons progress to the Holy Royal Arch, which is seen there as the completion of the Master Mason degree. The password for the Royal Arch is '*Ammi Ruhamah*' (My people have found mercy).

Under the Scottish Rite, which is widely followed in the United States,

candidates for the Royal Arch must first be Mark Masons. This is based on the identifying marks that medieval masons used to identify their work as their own. Mark Masonry is a separate degree that has its own Grand Lodge and subordinate lodges in England. It has around 6,000 members.

ROBES AND REGALIA

Centuries ago, when the cathedral builders of Europe were at work, it was usual for operative masons to wear a lambskin apron to protect their clothing underneath. Today's Masons continue to wear them, not to keep their clothes clean, but as a reminder that rich or poor, famous or anonymous, successful or struggling, in the eyes of Freemasonry all men are equal.

The unadorned white Apron of the First Degree represents the purity of the soul that the Apprentice strives for in attaining that degree. The pale blue rosettes added to the Apron in the Second Degree indicates that the candidate's spirituality is beginning to develop (pale blue is the colour of the sky and is traditionally associated with devotion to matters spiritual).

That fact that still further progress has been made by the time the Fellow Craft is raised to Master is symbolized not just by the increased blue ornamentation of the Master's Apron, but also by the silver tassels and the silver serpent (the symbol of Divine Wisdom) that is used to fasten the apron strings.

Officers of the Grand Lodge wear even more elaborately decorated aprons, symbolic of the even deeper spirituality that they have attained in being elected to office.

It was in 1914 that the Board of Works of the United Grand Lodge acted to standardize the patters on Masonic regalia and the jewels associated with each rank. Deviation from the prescribed designs was allowed only with the permission of the Grand Master.

Officers were provided with plain, undress garments as well as richly embroidered, full dress affairs, fringed with gold tassels and edged with garter blue and rich with Masonic symbols. It was such a grand one that President Washington wore when he laid the foundation stone of the Capitol Building in the city that bears his name.

At the same time, lodge officers were provided with emblems of their office to be worn from a sky-blue collar.

Today, with the proliferation of degrees around the world, particularly in the United States where the Scottish Rite is widely observed, and the Knights Templar a popular order, the designs of such emblems are rich and varied. There, as here, Master Masons may wear ornate chains of office, and as they proceed from degree to degree don appropriate robes of office.

A visit to one of the many shops that specialize in supplying Masonic jewels and regalia is a fascinating experience and not just for members of The Craft, but also for the 'layman'. There is a rich selection, not just of jewels and aprons, sashes and collars, but of pottery and engraved glass, ties, embossed leatherwork, diaries, books, medals and other memorabilia. But it is perhaps the jewels that are the most eye-catching.

Too many and various are the orders and too many and various are the jewels of each to identify them all. The ones described here are those that are worn by officers of the Grand Lodge. The emblems of each are cast from gold or another suitable yellow metal and are suspended within a golden circle.

The Past Grand Master wears a compass opened on a quarter circle with a triangle in the centre. The Master sports a similar one, but with a sun in the centre. The Senior Warden's jewel contains a square, while his Junior's has a level. It is crossed keys for the Treasurer, crossed pens for the Secretary and crossed swords for the Tylers..

Robes in glowing colours, heavy gold chains, silver, jewelled emblems of office – they all contribute to the richness of Freemasonry and hark back to the past when life was, perhaps, more colourful than it is today.

Regalia and adornments of the Grand Officer of the Grand Lodge of England. Regalia around the world does differ but the designs of the emblems are always rich and varied

IDEALS AND VIRTUES

From the moment he takes his first step in The Craft, the Freemason is taught to live his life, both in and out of the lodge, by a set of principles, ideals and virtues . . .

Whenever he is in a lodge, a Freemason of any standing cannot help but be conscious of the symbolism that is part and parcel of its fabric and furnishings. The lodge is symbolic of the universe, with the sun blazing its importance for all to gaze and wonder at.

The decorations in the Tracing Boards for each degree and the symbolic meaning of each of the tools serve to remind the Mason of the purpose of The Craft and the principles by which all lodge members are exhorted to live.

The most arresting of these symbols, the ones that no one can fail to notice on entering a lodge, are the three pillars of Wisdom, Strength and Beauty. They serve to represent the omniscience and omnipotence of the Supreme Being and the perfect symmetry of his (and few in The Craft would use any other pronoun) creation. They can be seen physically in the lodge as an Ionic, Doric and Corinthian columns, each one different in shape and form from the other, and also metaphorically as the senior officers of the lodge – the Master, the Senior and the Junior Warden. No lodge can be opened without their presence.

Not all Masons can hope to demonstrate the wisdom of such fellow Craftsmen as Benjamin Franklin and George Washington and other visionaries, who believed passionately in the wisdom of fighting for the freedom to live free from colonial rule. But, as one senior figure in Freemasonry in the United States has written, it is open to all Masons to strive to find the wisdom to see life simply and clearly, which is one of the most important gifts that The Craft can bestow on its members. 'We all make mistakes: Masonic wisdom encourages us not just to learn from them, but to judge our performance in every aspect of our lives against certain standards, adjust and move forwards, having learnt to compare their performance and their actions against a higher standard.'

MASONIC BUILDINGS

Strength and Beauty can be seen not just in the strength of character of many Freemasons, famous and unknown alike, but physically, too, in the buildings that are associated with The Craft: either via the men who built them or via the purpose for which they were built. London's St Paul's Cathedral, for instance, was designed by Christopher Wren, a Freemason, who worked on his masterpiece for over 30 years, after the original building was destroyed during the Great Fire of London in 1666. During the Second World War, it came to symbolize the strength of the British people, particularly Londoners, as they bore the brunt of Hitler's bombers.

Britain's capital is rich in other buildings designed by Freemasons. Nicholas Hawksmoor, Wren's assistant, designed several, which are among the most beautiful in London. Sir John Soane's design for the Bank of England resonates with Strength as well as Beauty. Sir Robert Smirke's famous British Museum has been rightly admired by countless visitors as they approach its imposing entrance. The eight pillars that support the triangular architrave combine Strength and Beauty, and with Minerva, the Greek goddess of Wisdom (one of the pantheon contained within the architrave) Smirke, a Freemason like Hawksmoor and Soane, succeeded in capturing the three ideals, Strength, Beauty and Wisdom, in one structure.

This design for an Italian Masonic Temple is a prime example of how such temples were all linked by common themes – in this case the pillars

Freemasons' Hall

One building in London that seeks to give physical expression to Strength and Beauty is Freemasons' Hall, in London. The present Hall is the third such building that has stood on the site in Great Queen Street since the Premier Grand Lodge bought the land in 1775.

The original purchase was a house that fronted the street, and behind it a large garden that backed onto a second house. The Grand Lodge decided to commission a Grand Hall, linking the front house – 'The Freemason's Arms' – with the one behind, which was to be used as offices and meeting rooms. A competition was announced; the eventual winner being the design proposed by Thomas Sandy.

As well as being used for Masonic purposes, Sandy's Grand Hall became a popular meeting place for upper-class London society, hosting as it did concerts and balls which were much patronized during 'the Season'. It also became an important debating chamber where such societies as the Anti-Slavery Society and the British and Foreign Bible Society held regular meetings.

Freemasons' Hall was extended in the 1820s to a design by Sir John Soane, but later in the century, during the 1860s, more property was acquired west of Sandy's Hall. A new building was commissioned to the design of Frederick Pepys Cockerell. Although he incorporated Sandy's Grand Hall in his severely classical design, Soane's addition was sadly lost.

Designed by Sir Christopher Wren, St Paul's Cathedral in London embodies Strength, one of the Masonic Ideals

A fire in 1883 caused structural damage to Sandy's Grand Hall, but it was not demolished until 1933. Cockerell's Freemasons' Hall was largely demolished around the same time to make way for the current building. Some of it survives today as part of the Connaught Rooms, the function suites that are popular venues for social events, and not just in Masonic circles.

Today's Freemasons' Hall is an imposing and important building. Grade 2 listed both inside and out, it is the only one of London's Art Deco buildings that has been preserved as built and which is still used for the purpose for which it was constructed. It covers a valuable piece of prime London real estate on the fringes of fashionable Covent Garden.

When it was built, it was intended not just as a venue for London lodge meetings and social events, but as a memorial to the 3,225 English Freemasons who died during the First World War, and was initially known as the Masonic Peace Memorial. In 1939, on the outbreak of the Second World War, it reverted to its original name – Freemasons' Hall.

The Grand Temple

This is central to the Hall and provides a meeting place for the Grand Chapter of the Grand Lodge; it is also the venue for the annual meetings of several Home Counties Provincial Grand Lodges. The Chamber, which can seat 1,700, is approached via bronze doors each weighing over 1.25 tonnes. The imposing room, whose perfect acoustic and clear sight lines make it a popular venue for concerts, is rich in Masonic symbolism. It is around 33 metres long, 27 metres wide and 19 metres high. The ceiling cove features figures representing the four cardinal virtues – Prudence, Temperance, Fortitude and Justice – along with the arms of HRH the Duke of Connaught, after whom the function suite is named. Connaught was installed as Grand Master in 1901, when his brother Edward resigned on acceding to the British throne.

The Masonic Memorial Shrine

When the competition for the Shrine's design was announced in 1925, it attracted over one hundred entries. The judges, under the chairmanship of Sir Edward Lutyens, selected ten designs, from which that submitted by H. V. Ashley and his partner Winton Newman was chosen. Work started in 1927 and took 6 years to complete.

The stained-glass window contained within it symbolizes the attainment of peace through sacrifice and shows the Angel of Peace carrying a model of the tower of the Peace Memorial building. The memorial casket contained within the Shrine is the work of Sir Gilbert Scott, who designed the memorial to Queen Victoria that faces Buckingham Palace; the statue of Peter Pan that stands in a leafy glade in Kensington Gardens; and the world-famous statue of Eros in Piccadilly Circus. The casket can be seen via a glass aperture supported by four gilded figures, each one representing one arm of the fighting services.

Paris

Another war memorial with strong Masonic connections can be found in Paris, France. Originally built as a triumphal celebration of Napoleon's victories, the Arc de Triomphe was built to the design of French Freemason Jean-Francois Chalgrin. Beneath its huge 50 metre-plus arch burns an eternal flame, which marks the final resting place of France's Unknown Soldier.

The names of famous Freemasons also grace Paris' streets. When Napoleon III ordered the broad boulevards that are such a feature of the city to be built in the 1860s, he named them after several of Napoleon's marshals. Of these successful soldiers, three were active in military lodges, five were Grand Officers of the Grand Orient and seven held high rank in the Ancient and Accepted Scottish Rite. In naming the boulevards after these men, Napoleon was not only trying to attract some of his uncle's glory to himself, but was paying a tribute to Freemasonry.

The Arc de Triomphe, one of the structures in Paris that has strong Masonic overtones

The United States

Across the Atlantic in the United States, several of the most famous buildings in the capital are the work of Freemasons. They include the Capitol Building in Washington as well the White House. The first presidential residence in the capital, a wooden structure built in traditional colonial style was designed by James Hoban, who founded Federal Lodge No. 1 at Washington, DC. After the building was destroyed by fire by the British during the war of 1812, Hoban designed the one with which we are familiar today.

One of the most beautiful buildings in Baltimore, the Roman Catholic Cathedral, is the work of Benjamin Latrobe, the Freemason often called, 'the Father of American Architecture'. Latrobe was the man who designed most of the Capitol Building after it met the same fate as the original White House in 1812.

A century later, in Chicago, north of Washington, Daniel Burnham, the architect who was one of the most visionary Freemasons, architecturally speaking, was hard at work. In 1909, he presented his 'Plan of Chicago', which was a blueprint for his ideal city and one of the first plans for a modern regional metropolis. The plan was never realized, but the Masonic Temple he designed for the city in 1892 was genuinely awe-inspiring. Visitors to New York can see an example of his work on downtown Broadway, where the Flatiron Building remains one of the city's most remarkable structures. When it was built in 1903, it towered around fifteen storeys above its neighbours, however today it would not come anywhere near being included in a list of the one of the 100 highest buildings in New York. Burnham, had he still been alive, would not complain: the skyscrapers he pioneered have changed the face of the world.

Freemasons' Hall in London, shown here as it was in the early nineteenth century, has been used by Masons and non-Masons alike for many different purposes

MASONS AND THE ARTS

In the visual arts, such men as the English cartoonist William Hogarth, the Italian engraver Francesco Bartolozzi, the Czech painter and illustrator Alphonse Muncha, the Spanish Cubist Juan Gris, the French Modernist Marc Chagall and a host of others – painters, designers and craftsmen, silversmiths, furniture makers and bookbinders – were all enthusiastic Freemasons. And while he was not a Freemason himself, William Blake was obviously inspired by the symbols of The Craft and incorporated them into his own symbolism.

There have been and still are many Masons involved in popular music, including the velvet-voiced Nat 'King' Cole, bandleader and composer Duke Ellington and his fellow jazzman Count Basie. One of the greatest hits enjoyed by a member of Lodge Montgomery No 18, Prince Hall Affiliation, New York could serve as an anthem to Freemasons' attitude to the arts. The song was 'What a Wonderful World.' The singer was Louis Armstrong, one of many famous men from the world of the arts who have been Freemasons. And on the classical front, the prolific symphonist Joeseph Haydn was a Freemason.

The grandest lodge in Vienna in Haydn's day was *Zur Wohltaigkeit* (Charity) but Haydn was a member of one of the city's smaller lodges, *Zur Wahren Eintracht* (True Harmony). It was Haydn who introduced another famous Austrian composer to Freemasonry: Wolfgang Amadeus Mozart.

A meeting of the Viennese Lodge that counted Wolfgang Amadeus Mozart among its members. The great composer wrote many pieces of music specifically to be performed at this and other Lodges

THE MAGIC FLUTE

Sources disagree as to which lodge Mozart was entered into. Some say it was into the grand *Zur Wohltaigkeit*, where he was sponsored by one of Vienna's leading aristocrats. Others claim that Haydn sponsored him for membership of his own lodge.

Whichever, most agree that it was in *Zur Wahren Eintracht* that the young composer received his Fellow Craft degree in January 1785, and 3 months later he became a Master Mason.

Mozart, not just one of the greatest of composers but also one of the most prolific, wrote several pieces specifically to be played in Masonic lodges, others for the general public built on Masonic themes and yet more that were adapted to be played in lodges. Into the first category fall the Adagio for two clarinets and three horns K.411, which was written to be played during the processional entrance into the Lodge, and *Die Gesellenreise: Die ihr einem neuen grade* K.429, which Mozart wrote in honour of his father, Leopold, being made Fellow Craft. Into the third group come the Adagio and Fugue in C Minor K.546 and the motet *Ave Verum Corpus* K.618m, which was originally written for a choir school in Baden, but which was soon being played in lodges all over Germany and Austria.

Into the second category falls one of the most famous of all operas. The idea for it came from the librettist Johann Emanuel Schikaneder, himself an ardent Freemason, who, like most Austrian lodge members, had been dismayed by the empress Marie Theresa's attitude towards the Brethren.

When she died in 1780, her son Joseph came to the imperial throne. Much more liberal than his formidable mother, Joseph was more relaxed than her in his attitude towards Freemasonry. Indeed, it became so fashionable in Vienna that modish

The Austrian emperor, Leopold II. It was to celebrate his coronation as king of Bohemia that Mozart wrote The Magic Flute

women ordered their dressmakers to incorporate the Masons' apron and other emblems into the dresses they ordered, and for a time it was *de rigueur* to sport white gloves, something which had and still has strong Masonic connections.

But Joseph's attitude towards the Freemasons was to change, thanks to the activities of a secret society known as the Illuminati. Founded by Adam Weishaupt, who had been born into a Jewish family but baptized into the Roman Catholic Church, the Illuminati began its life as a small band of five members, which grew to around 2,500 when the society was at its height. The shared aim of the Illuminati was ambitious – the overthrow of all governments, secular and religious alike, to be replaced by a regime based on tolerance and universal liberty.

With their shared disapproval of religious persecution and desire for understanding between men of different views in matters of religion, Weishaupt saw what he thought was a common bond between his Illuminati and Freemasonry and decided to infiltrate The Craft.

Unfortunately for the Austrian Freemasons, Weishaupt was denounced for peddling seditious and blasphemous propaganda in Bavaria where he was Professor of Canon Law at Ingoldstadt University. When he was expelled from his post, he fled Bavaria in such haste that he left behind documents that made clear his movement's aims and ambitions. When these were published by the Bavarian government they caused a sensation.

Joseph's reaction was to issue an edict, in December 1785, declaring that the information he had concerning Freemasonry showed that it was a beneficial organization. But, he wrote, there was a danger that being essentially the meeting places of a secret society, Masonic lodges could be used by some members as a cloak for the promotion of revolution. He therefore decreed that no province in his empire should have more than one lodge, exceptions being made for Vienna, Budapest and Prague, where three lodges each were to be permitted.

Joseph died in 1790 and was succeeded by his brother Leopold. By then both the American War of Independence and French Revolution had happened, and there were many who detected the hand of the Freemasons behind both. Among them was Marie Antoinette, Leopold's sister, by now a prisoner of the Revolution in the Tuilleries, in Paris. It was from there that she wrote to her brother, 'Take good care over there about any organization of Freemasons.'

The doomed queen was not the only one to warn Leopold about the activities of the Masons. His chiefs of police and his bishops were openly hostile to the Craft, too.

Leopold's coronation as king of Bohemia was scheduled for September 1791, and Schikaneder knew that Mozart would be expected to compose a work for the opera company there to mount in celebration of the event. As one Freemason to another, Schikaneder suggested to Mozart that he should use this as an opportunity to write an opera that would show Freemasonry in a good light.

And that is how *The Magic Flute* came about.

At the start of the opera, Prince Tamino is rescued from a serpent by the three ladies who serve the Queen of the Night, but a birdcatcher, Papageno, takes the credit for slaying the monster. As a punishment for lying, the women padlock his mouth before giving Tamino a painting of the Queen's daughter, Pamina, who is being held captive by the evil Sorastro. Opera being opera, he falls in love with the girl in the picture and sets off to rescue her, with Papageno accompanying him . . .

All ends well for the lovebirds and by the final curtain, it is the Queen and her ladies who are found to be the evil ones and are engulfed in a clap of thunder, while the others celebrate the victory of light over darkness, which is in itself significant to Freemasonry.

In between, Sorastro is found to be the ruler of the Temple of Wisdom, which is supported by three pillars, into whose mysteries Tamino asks to be initiated. To do so, he has to undergo trial by darkness, silence, circumspection, privation, fire and water. Tamino passes, but Papageno fails, but is rewarded nonetheless, having made the wise decision to be led by those who have acquired wisdom.

The similarities to the ceremonies and rituals of Freemasonry are quite clear. Also, the use of the E-flat, G and B-flat triad in the music (the opera's opening chords sound three times) and the many references to the figure 'three' can hardly be accidental, given its significance to Freemasonry.

In the opera the Queen of the Night has three ladies; there are three boys who serve as guides to Tamino and Papageno; and Tamino makes three attempts to open the three doors of the three temples (Wisdom, Truth and Reason).

In Freemasonry, there are the three degrees of Apprentice, Fellow Craft and Master Mason. The lodge stands east to west for three reasons, and is supported by the three pillars of Wisdom, Strength and Beauty. There are three movable jewels (the tracing board, the rough ashlar and the perfect ashlar), the three immovable jewels (the square, level and plumb) and the three principles of Brotherly Love, Relief and Truth.

The opera was first staged in September 1791. Mozart, exhausted by working on it simultaneously with his *Requiem*, died a few weeks afterwards. His legacy to us is some of the most beautiful music ever written, and, thanks to *The Magic Flute*, one with which all Freemasons can identify.

THE VIRTUES OF THE CRAFT

Many people see Freemasons as little more than a group of men who meet in secret, partake in secret rituals and whose ultimate aim is to look after each other.

Nothing could be further from the truth.

From the moment an Apprentice is entered into a lodge, it is impressed upon him that his duty is not to himself, but to his family and his fellow man, his community and his country.

Inherent in living by the precepts of Brotherly Love, Relief and Truth is the duty to be tolerant in respecting the right of others to hold beliefs that are different to his. So the Freemason must *be tolerant*.

The committed Freemason must do whatever he can to improve society, and that

is why members of The Craft have helped found schools and colleges, hospitals and libraries. To enable them to do this they must *strive to achieve*.

Millions of pounds, dollars, francs, marks, kroner and now euros have been raised by Freemasons over the years, all over the world and donated to charities large and small. In one year alone (1990) British Freemasons disbursed £18 million to Masonic charities, while on the other side of the Atlantic, their American brothers raised similar sums, much of it donated to the sick and the elderly.

No natural disaster occurs without Freemasons making substantial donations to emergency appeals for funds. From as long ago as 1871, when fire swept through Chicago, to as recently as 2004 when a terrible tsunami engulfed many Indian Ocean countries and killed over 250,000 men, women and children, Freemasons have dug deep into their pockets and donated to the necessary charities.

It goes without saying that to live up to the ideals of The Craft, Freemasons must live a life of *integrity*, and that they must be *faithful* to their lodges and fellow Freemasons.

These five virtues – tolerance, achievement, charity, integrity and fidelity – are the backbone of the Freemasons' way of life.

The world would be a better place if more of us accepted them as the watchwords by which to live our own lives.

A set design for an 1816 production of The Magic Flute. *The figure atop the crescent Moon is the villainous Queen of the Night, based on the empress Maria Theresa, who members of The Craft viewed as an enemy*

Sir Winston Churchill, Britain's great World War II leader, followed his father, Lord Randolph Churchill, into The Craft

FAMOUS FREEMASONS

Many Freemasons were already well known both in their specialist fields and to the public at large when they were entered into the Craft. A host of others became famous after they become Lodge members – perhaps helped on the way by their fellows . . .

No one has (or at least no one is known to have) collected the records of all the men who have been accepted as Freemasons since 1717 when the Goose and Gridiron hosted what could be called the inaugural meeting of the Grand Lodge. If anyone were to undertake such a task, the list would run into millions of names. Most of these are lost to history, but there are thousands whose names linger. Like their now unknown brethren, they all followed three great principles.

First they were all taught to show tolerance and respect for the opinions of others and to behave with kindness and understanding to their fellow men (and women): several words that can be summed up in two, brotherly love.

Second, they were all taught to practise charity and to care not only for their own, but also for the community as a whole. They were encouraged to give to charity and to work both together and as individuals for the common good. This principle of relief is one that has concerned Freemasons since the early days, since when they have provided funds for the care of orphans, the sick and the aged and have raised huge sums of money for national and local charities. That they often do so unasked for and unheralded is something that has stood, stands and will continue to stand to their enormous credit.

Third, and perhaps the most important thing that all Masons, famous and unknown, are taught is that they must strive for Truth. Being a Freemason requires the highest moral standards, and all who are accepted into The Craft must aim to live their lives by such standards. Failure to be anything less than 100 per cent truthful at all times lets down not just the individual but also the whole Freemasonry brotherhood.

Among the names that follow are British kings, scientists and others, all of whom were keen to be accepted as Masons. Once initiated, nearly all lived their lives by the standards expected of all Freemasons, regardless of class or creed. Most of them, that is; there were one or two of them who disappointingly failed to live up to the standards expected.

Edwin 'Buzz' Aldrin It would have been nice to record that the first name on this list was the first man to walk on the Moon, but there is no record of Neil Armstrong having been accepted into The Craft. However, the man who was just a few steps behind him, 'Buzz' Aldrin, was initiated into a lodge in New Jersey several years before he followed Neil Armstrong down the ladder and on to the surface of our nearest neighbour in space.

Salvador Allende had been a mason for 35 years before he was elected president of Chile in 1970. when he was in his early sixties. He was assassinated 3 years later during the military coup that ended democratic rule in the country for several years.

Buzz' Aldrin, the second man to walk on the surface of the Moon, was entered into a New Jersey Lodge several years before he became world famous

Sir Edward Appleton, the Nobel Prize winner whose experiments led to the discovery of the ionosphere, was initiated into Cambridge's Isaac Newton Lodge in 1922 and was an active member throughout his lifetime.

Louis 'Satchmo' Armstrong was a member of a New York lodge. Today, more then 30 years after his death, his name remains in the pantheon of jazz 'greats'. He is remembered as one of the best jazz trumpet players and a singer equally at home with up tempo 'scat' singing and sentimental ballads.

Thomas Arne, the man who is best known as the composer of *Rule Britannia*, also wrote two operas, several oratorios and set to music *Under the Greenwood Tree, Where the Bee Sucks* and other songs featured in Shakespeare's plays.

Charles Ashbee was, like Edward Appleton, a member of the Isaac Newton Lodge in Cambridge where he was initiated in 1900. Ashbee was also one of the Arts and Crafts Movement's leading lights. He bought William Morris's printing presses and established the Essex House Press.

John Jacob Astor, the German-born American financier who invested the fortune he made in the fur trade in New York property and made an even larger one, was a member of New York City's Holland Lodge No. 8.

John James Audobon, the American ornithologist and artist whose book *Birds of America* is considered a masterpiece, referred to himself in his diary as 'Mason' and 'Brother', but there are no records as to which of America's many lodges he belonged to.

Sir Joseph Banks, who was appointed president of Britain's Royal Society in 1778 and retained the position until he died in 1829, was an enthusiastic Freemason. From 1768 until 1771, he circumnavigated the world with Captain Cook aboard *Endeavour*. He presented the botanical specimens he collected during the voyage to the Royal Botanic Gardens at Kew, laying the foundations of making it the internationally renowned institution it is today.

Frederic Bartholdi designed the Statue of Liberty. The statue, a gift to the people of the United States from France to commemorate the centenary of US Independence (and properly called *Liberty Enlightening the World*) was an enthusiastic Freemason and influential in the decision to mark its opening with a full Freemasonic ceremony.

Irving Berlin, the Russian-born songwriter who wrote *Annie Get Your Gun* and several other Broadway hits, and whose song 'White Christmas' is one of the best sellers of all time, was a member of New York City's Munn Lodge No. 190. True to his Masonic ideals, he gave the not-insubstantial royalties of several of his songs to a charity for deprived youngsters. On his hundredth birthday in 1988, thousands of New Yorkers, including many of those his gesture had helped, stood outside his Manhattan apartment and serenaded him with several choruses of 'Happy Birthday to You!' – a song he didn't write.

Louis Armstrong – singer, trumpeter and Freemason

Simón Bolivar, the dashing 'George Washington of the South', who liberated much of South America from Spanish rule, entered The Craft while he was living in Cadiz in Spain in 1807. Seventeen years later, he founded Peru's Lodge Order and Liberty No. 2.

Edmund Burke, the Irish-born British statesman and philosopher, was one of England's foremost political thinkers at the time when the American colonies were demanding independence and later when the French were demanding their king's head. He was for the former and against the latter. Burke enthusiastically embraced the ideals of Freemasonry in his political thought.

Robert Burns, Scotland's national poet, was initiated into St David's Lodge No. 174 in 1781 when he was 22 and later became an enthusiastic member of at least two other lodges in his native country. There are several specific references to Freemasonry in his work, which he used to express his profound dislike of rank hypocrisy and his belief that 'man to man, the world o'er will brothers be, for a' that'.

Perhaps not such a leading light as many of his fellow Freemasons, Casanova lends some colour to the line-up of famous Freemasons

Michael Caine, the Oscar-winning actor who shot to fame as the original 'Alfie' and followed this with memorable screen performances in classics such as *Funeral in Berlin*, *Hannah and Her Sisters* and *Cider House Rules*, is one of many famous actors to have been entered into a Masonic lodge.

Winston Churchill, Britain's prime minister for much of the Second World War, was the embodiment of Strength, one of the three Masonic Ideals. At a time when Britain alone among the European countries was standing up against Hitler, Churchill's indomitable spirit and refusal to submit was a strong factor in the winning of the war.

Jack Dempsey, as well as holding the World Heavyweight Boxing Championship from 1919 to 1926, was also a member of Chicago's Kenwood Lodge No. 800.

Sir Arthur Conan Doyle, creator of perhaps the most famous fictional detective of all time, Sherlock Holmes, entered The Craft at Portsmouth in 1893.

Edward VII had to wait such a long time to inherit the throne – he was 60 when his mother, Queen Victoria died – that it is hardly surprising he spent much of the waiting years devoting himself to pleasure, particularly that offered by beautiful women. And as beauty is one of the five virtues, perhaps we should not be so unkind to him. As Prince of Wales he was Grand Master of the United Grand Lodge for more than a quarter of a century, from 1875. He relinquished the honour on coming to the throne in 1901.

Edward VIII, Edward VII's grandson, is best known as the king who, because he could not rule without the woman he loved (a twice-divorced, poker-playing beauty) by his side, gave up the British throne for her. Like his great-great-great uncle William IV he probably became a Freemason when he was serving in the Royal Navy. He may have had his faults, but he was concerned with the plight of the working man, and when he witnessed the dreadful conditions in which many poor people in Britain lived demanded that something be done. Two of his brothers, and one brother-in-law were also members of the Craft.

George IV, the British king who, as Prince Regent from 1810 to 1820, was acknowledged as the most stylish man of his generation, is said to have been a Freemason. If he was, he was one of The Craft's black sheep: he loathed his father, was unfaithful to his wife (to be fair he had been forced into a loveless marriage) and was an unloving father. But he is said to have had impeccable manners and was acknowledged as the 'first gentleman of Europe'.

Giovanni Jacopo Casanova de Seingalt, better known by his third name alone and best known for his prodigious sexual appetite, was made a Mason around 1750 when he was living in Lyon in France.

William IV was George IV's (see above) younger brother and came to the British throne on George's death in 1830. Like his brother, he seems to have paid little heed to the tenets of Freemasonry, into which he was probably initiated when he was a serving officer in the British navy. He fathered at least ten illegitimate children and was firmly against the extension of the franchise, the abolition of colonial slavery and the reform of the Poor Laws.

WOMEN IN FREEMASONRY

Women are barred from Freemasonry, but in the United States and other countries there are Masonic-like organizations that are open to women, many of whose husbands, fathers or brothers are members of The Craft...

e have already seen, in Chapter 4, that 250 years ago in Europe, there was a fashion for Lodges of Adoption, which were conducted by regular Masonic lodges and to which women were admitted and took part in elaborate ersatz Masonic rituals. In the nineteenth century, Napoleon's first wife, Josephine Beauharnais, served as the Grand Mistress of such a lodge, the Saint Caroline Lodge of Adoption.

EUROPE

Lodges of Adoption worked a system of three degrees, Apprentice, Fellow Craft and Mistress Mason. They based their symbolism on the Book of Genesis, and drew their moral lessons from the legends of Noah's Ark, Jacob's Ladder and the Tower of Babel.

But such lodges as these were essentially frivolous affairs, as can be assumed from the name of one of them, the Order of Mopses, founded in Vienna after the anti-Masonic papal bull was issued in 1738. The Order was open to Roman Catholic men and women and took its name from the pug breed of dog, which was regarded as a token of the fidelity and attachment that existed between members.

Five years after the papal bull, a Freemason called John Coustous, who lived in Lisbon, was asked by the Portuguese Inquisition why women were not admitted to The Craft. His reply would surely be seen as offensive in today's climate of equality between the sexes:

> *The reason why women are excluded from the Society is to take away all occasion of calumny and reproach, which would have been unavoidable had they been admitted into it. Further, that since women have, in general, always been considered as not very well qualified to keep a secret: the founders of the Society of Freemasons by their exclusion of the other sex, thereby give a signal proof of their prudence and wisdom.*

But there are several instances of women gaining admission into regular Masonic lodges. In 1713, a young Irish woman, Elizabeth St Leger, accidentally came across a lodge meeting in her father's house in County Cork. The men promptly made her a Mason and she later took the Apprentice and Fellow Craft Degrees. Had the Master's Degree existed at the time, there is no reason to suppose she would not have been raised to it, for she regarded herself as a true Mason for the rest of her life, and was treated as one by her brethren.

At the time there was no widespread clamour for women to become active members of The Craft because the various constitutions forbade it. But in 1882, in

Josephine de Beauharnais, Napoleon's first wife, served as Grand Matraisse du Loge d'Adoption Sainte-Caroline. Women were admitted by regular Masonic lodges and participated in rituals that were often elaborate in the extreme

France, when the Grand Independent Symbolic Lodge decided to go its own way from the Supreme Council of France, the members of one lodge, *Les Libres Penseurs* (The Free Thinkers) decided to admit one ardent feminist, Maria Desraimes, into their number. The initiation, which was illegal under the French Masonic constitution, took place in the small town of Le Pecq, near Paris. Mlle Desraimes later passed Free Craft and was raised to *Maitresse*.

When word got out, the Grand Lodge immediately suspended *Les Libres Penseurs* from its ranks and the lady was left as a Masonic outcast. But in 1892 she was

approached by a member or the Supreme Council, Dr Georges Martin, a fervent believer in the equality of the sexes, who suggested to her that they establish a lodge that would be open to Masons of both sexes.

In the early months of the following year, Mlle Desraimes (she never accepted the custom of women of a certain age styling themselves *Madame* regardless of their marital status) initiated, passed and raised sixteen women, all of whom became members of the new lodge, *Le Droit Humain* (The Human Duty). The lodge was the only one belonging to the newly constituted *Grande Loge Symbolique Ecossaise Mixte de France* (The Grand Symbolic Mixed Scottish Rite of France).

At first, the lodge worked only the three degrees of the traditional Craft, but as time passed and it attracted more and more members, so the demand for additional degrees grew. In 1900, 7 years after it was founded, a Supreme Council came into being, charged with the government of the Order, which decided to work the 33 degrees of the Ancient and Accepted Scottish Rite.

LODGES IN BRITAIN

Among the women who flocked to join the new Order was Annie Besant, who, in 1902, brought mixed or co-Masonry to Britain, promoting it among members of her Theosophical Society, where it was known as 'Joint Freemasonry'. Three years later she changed its name to 'Universal Co-Freemasonry', taking for herself the title 'Grand Master of the Supreme Council'.

Besant was an extraordinary woman. A passionate believer in birth control (she risked imprisonment for co-authoring a pamphlet promoting it), she was a genuine free-thinker, and if lodge meetings over which she presided

Annie Besant, the woman who brought mixed Masonry to Britain. Despite the force of her extraordinary personality, it was never accepted into the mainstream of traditional Freemasonry

were any reflection of her character, they must have been lively to say the least. She was also, along with Bernard Shaw and Beatrice and Sydney Webb, also a member of the Fabian Society, which was at the forefront of the foundation of the British Labour Party.

In 1908, the movement experienced the first of several schisms. Among the organizations that came into existence as a result of the schism was the Honourable Fraternity of Ancient Freemasonry, which was founded in 1913. Its first Grand Master was Elizabeth Boswell-Reid, who held the office for 20 years, when she was succeeded by her daughter, Mrs Seton Challen.

Based in London, the Honourable Fraternity continues to exist, and like other similar quasi-Masonic organizations, some exclusive to women and others open to men and women, hold regular lodge meetings, organize social functions. Like the Freemasons, who they regard as brothers, they also raise large amounts of money for charity.

But regular Masonry recognizes neither mixed orders nor those that admit only women to their rank. As far as traditional Masons are concerned The Craft has always been a male bastion and they intend that it will always be so.

ACROSS THE ATLANTIC

Almost half a century before Maria Desraimes founded her Order, across the Atlantic, the Order of the Eastern Star was founded in 1850. Open to Master Masons and 'their ladies' it is the largest organization of its kind. Unlike other similar organizations, such as the Royal Arch Widows and the Daughters of the Nile to name but two that are mainly social, fund-raising organizations, the Eastern Star is a serious in intent, and in its teaching and its ceremonials.

The Order was founded by Dr Robert Morris, a Boston-born lawyer who was a Master Mason and had been Past Grand Master of Kentucky. He had intended to found a female branch of Freemasonry, but opposition was so intense that the organization he eventually founded was, and is, open to men and women.

The Grand Chapter, with its headquarters at the Eastern Star Temple in Washington, DC, grants charters to state-level Grand Chapters who control the organization within their territories. Members must be at least 18 and either a Master Mason in 'good standing' or properly related to one such. The second category originally included wives, widows, sisters (and half-sisters), daughter, mothers, granddaughters, step-mothers, sisters and daughters. In 1994 this was expanded to include nieces, daughters and grandmothers. In short, more or less any woman with a family tie to a Master Mason (apart from a mistress) is eligible for membership.

There are eighteen officers in each chapter, some elected and others appointed by elected officials. By constitution, the Patron and the Associate Patron have to be male. The presiding office of each chapter is the Worthy Matron, but degrees cannot be conferred without either the Patron or his Associate being in attendance.

Each chapter holds the right to decide who shall be elected to membership, and election through the five degrees, which are conferred in one ceremony, must be unanimous, decided without debate and voted for in secret. Every member has to profess a belief in the Supreme Being, which, while not being specifically barred, makes it difficult for non-Christians to belong to the Order.

As long ago as 1874, the Order of the Eastern Star established its first chapter for black women in the United States, and today such chapters as the Queen Esther and the Queen of Sheba, among many others, are actively involved in charity work along with their white Sisters coast to coast.

THE NEXT GENERATION

Young people have not been ignored by Freemasonry in the United States, where several chapters of such organizations as The Order of de Molay (named after a Knight Templar), The Order of the Rainbow and The Order of Job's Daughters are sponsored by Masonic lodges. Belonging to such an order is no guarantee that its members will automatically be accepted into an adult lodge. But in promoting responsible citizenship and encouraging their members to look out for others not as fortunate as themselves, such orders ensure that the ideals of Freemasonry will be handed down from generation to generation. And that, surely, can only be a good thing in a world that has become progressively individualistic.

Some of the regalia associated with the French Woman's Grand Lodge. In most Rites, Freemasonery is exclusively male, but in France, in 1893, a lodge that admitted women to membership was founded

GLOSSARY

A complete glossary of the Masonic terms would run to many more pages than are available here. Robert Macoy's excellent *A Dictionary of Freemasonry*, still in print after it was published in the last years of the nineteenth century, for example, runs to 700 pages of fascinating detail. From its first entry, Aaron (the brother of Moses) to its last, Zerubbabel (to whom was entrusted the care of the vessels of the Temple in Jerusalem), the tome is packed with more than even the most dedicated of Freemasons would need to know.

Accepted Mason. In modern times, a Freemason: originally a non-operative man who was accepted into a lodge of operative masons.

Additional Degrees. The Grand Lodge of England recognizes three degrees: Apprentice, Fellow Craft and Master Mason (including the Royal Arch). In other countries, particularly the United States, members can advance to up to as many 33 Degrees, which are referred to as higher or additional.

Adoptive Masonry. Continental Orders into which women were admitted during the eighteenth and nineteenth centuries.

Advancement. A term applied to a candidate when he is invested with the degree of Mark Master as he moves towards the Royal Arch.

Allied Masonic Degrees. Degrees which until 1880 were unconnected and had no governing body. In that year, a Grand Council of the Allied Masonic Degrees was founded in England to govern these degrees, which today include St Lawrence the Martyr, the Red Cross of Babylon and the Grand Tylers of Solomon. In the United States, such degrees are governed by a Grand Council.

Ancient and Accepted (Scottish) Rite. Referred to outside the United Kingdom as the Scottish Rite, a system of 33 degrees that evolved out of the eighteenth-century, 25-degree French Rite of Perfection.

Apprentice A First Degree member who has been entered into The Craft but has still to be passed as Fellow Craft and beyond. Properly called an Entered Apprentice.

Apron. Worn by operative masons to protect their clothes, the apron was adopted by Accepted Masons as the principal item of the Freemasons' regalia and must be worn at all lodge meetings. They were originally made of lambskin, but the ones worn today are crafted from cloth. As a Freemason progresses through the degrees, he is entitled to wear more and more elaborately designed aprons, the design of which denote the degree achieved and the office attained.

Ashlar. A building stone which in its rough form is symbolic of the Apprentice, and when it has been worked and is considered perfect is the state he hopes to achieve by living his life according to the tenets of The Craft.

Book of Constitution. The basic rules and regulations by which a Grand Lodge operates and governs the lodges loyal to it.

Bourn. An archaic term for the boundary of a lodge.

Brought to Light. The moment when a candidate for Entering, Passing or Raising has his hoodwink removed.

Cable tow. The rope by which a candidate for Advancement is led into the lodge.

Capitular Masonry. A term sometimes used in the United States for Royal Arch Masonry.

Chapter. The basic unit of Royal Arch Freemasonry and sometimes used as a sobriquet for it.

Charges. The duties that a Freemason owes to his Supreme Being, society at large and the family in particular. The Charges relevant to each degree are explained to candidates for Initiation, Passing and Raising during the appropriate ceremony.

Clandestine lodge. One that meets without the authority of a recognized Masonic body and whose members would not be admitted to a properly authorized lodge.

Co-Masonry. Founded in Continental Europe towards the end of the nineteenth century and open to men and women, Co-Masonry spread from there to the United Kingdom and thence to the United States where it has a substantial following, despite the fact that it is not recognized by regular Freemasons.

Companions. Members of the Royal Arch, the term being used to distinguish them from Craft Masons.

Constitution. The rules that govern an Order of Freemasons. Lodges loyal to the United Grand Lodge of England are said to belong to the English Constitution just as lodges in Scotland, Ireland or wherever that are governed by the appropriate Grand Lodge belong to its Constitution.

Cowan. An accidental or deliberate intruder into a lodge.

Craft. Freemasonry as practised in lodges authorized by a Grand Lodge, as opposed to other Masonic Orders and Degrees.

Deacon. One of the Craft Lodge officers who assist the Worshipful Master to carry out his duties by acting as messengers and conducting candidates for initiation, passing or raising.

Degrees. The stages by which a Freemason progresses from Apprenticeship towards Master (in Craft Freemasonry) and beyond (in other Orders).

District Grand Lodge. The body in the English and Scottish traditions that governs the activities of lodges loyal to those traditions within a specific area. District Grand Lodges are headed by a District Grand Master. Thus the District Grand Master for New Zealand is the head Mason in that country's District Grand Lodge.

Eastern Star. A Co-Masonic Order founded in the United States by Robert Morris in the middle of the nineteenth century.

Entered Apprentice. *See* Apprentice.

Fellow Craft. The second degree in Freemasonry, having been passed from Entered Apprentice but not raised to Master.

Festive Board. The food and drink served after the formal business of a lodge meeting has been concluded, and where loyal and Masonic toasts are made.

Freemason. A member of a lodge loyal to an appropriate Grand Lodge. Freemasons are accepted rather than practising masons.

Grand Architect of the Universe. The Supreme Being in any religion, Christianity, Islam, etc. Because he is a common rather than a separate Masonic God, Masons of different religions aand faiths can acknowledge The Grand Architect without offending their own – or others' – religious scruples.

Grand Chapter. Organized on a national or, in the United States, state basis, the governing, supreme body of a group of Royal Arch Chapters. In the United States, there is a General Grand Chapter, which is an umbrella body to which some, but not all State Royal Arch Grand Chapters belong. Mainly a discussion body, the General Grand Chapter has no executive power to force its decisions on its member Chapters. Such decisions have to be voted on by individual Grand Chapters before they are adopted.

Grand Lodge. The final authority and governing body of a group of lodges. A Grand Lodge is a non-elective body, membership of which is by Masonic status or right of office. The laws it lays down must be adopted by member lodges, over which it has sovereign authority.

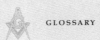

Grand Master. The senior member and constitutional ruler of a Grand Lodge, whose time in office is limited by the laws governing the lodge.

Grand Architect of the Universe (G.A.O.T.U). The term used by Freemasons to refer to the Supreme Being. Also called The Grand Geometrician of the Universe.

Grand Orient. The governing body of French Freemasonry. It is effectively an alternative expression for Grand Lodge and as such has been adopted by other European and South American bodies as the name they give to their governing body.

Higher Degrees. The 30th, 31st, 32nd and 33rd Degrees of the Ancient and Accepted (Scottish) Rite.

Hiram-Abiff. King Solomon's chief architect in building the Temple in Jerusalem. Reputedly murdered by three fellowcrafts when he refused to give them the secret word of a Master Mason. Within a lodge, he is associated with the Pillar of Strength, the West and the office of Senior Warden.

Hoodwink. The blindfold used put the wearer into a state of symbolic darkness during Degree ceremonies.

Immediate Past Master. The Master whose time in office has just expired and who has handed over to the present Master. As he has held that office, he is entitled to assume the chair at lodge meetings should the Master be unable to be present.

Immovable Jewels. The square, the level and the plumb which belong permanently and immovably to the three principal officers (Master and Senior and Junior Wardens) and their respective chairs.

Inner Guard. The lodge officer who stands guard inside the lodge door.

Jewels. The badges of rank and office, and the other medals sported by Masons. The rules governing the jewels that each rank and officer can wear are laid down by the Grand Lodge.

Knights Templar. A Masonic order taking its name from the organization founded in the twelfth century to protect pilgrims travelling to the Holy City of Jerusalem. Membership is restricted to practising Christians. In common with other Masonic orders, it has raised huge sums of money for charity.

Lewis. The son of a Freemason, named after the metal clamp that was inserted into a large stone by working masons to enable them to move it.

Lodge. A group of Freemasons authorized by the Grand Lodge and Grand Master to practise Freemasonry at regular meetings.

Mark Masonry. In some systems, part of the Royal Arch. In England, an extra degree with its own Grand Lodge that has authority over the lodges loyal to it.

Master. The senior office of a lodge and the official who presides over lodge meetings. In The Craft, the Master is elected to office by members of his lodge and rules for a period of one year. In some other systems, the Master is elected for life or until he decides to retire. Usually called Worshipful Master.

Master Mason. The third degree in The Craft, which is the final step to becoming a Freemason, at which point the offices of the lodge and advancement towards Master become possible.

Mother Lodge. The lodge in which a Freemason was introduced to The Craft.

Movable Jewels. The rough ashlar, the perfect ashlar and the tracing board.

Obligations. The promises made by Freemasons that they will uphold the principles of The Craft and keep secret the signs and passwords made known to them at entering, being passed or being raised.

Operative Mason. A working stone mason who prepared stone to be used in building.

Passing. The Second Degree ceremony in a lodge when an Entered Apprentice is admitted to the Fellow Craft degree.

Past Master. A Freemason who has served as Master of his lodge and who can chair a lodge meeting if the present Master is unable to attend.

Provincial Lodges. Lodges approved by the Grand Lodge to authorize junior lodges within the area over which their jurisdiction extends. The presiding officer of these lodges is Provincial Grand Master who is appointed by the Grand Master and is authorized to act as his deputy within the Province.

Quarterly Communication. The three-monthly meeting of a Grand Lodge at which administrative business is conducted.

Raising. The Third Degree ceremony at which a Fellow Craft is raised to Master Mason rank.

Royal Arch. In the English tradition, the final stage of the Master Mason degree. In other traditions, a separate degree. Common to both is that Companions of the Royal Arch are encouraged to dwell upon their relationship with whichever God or Supreme Being they believe in.

Shriner. A member of the Ancient Arabic Order of Nobles of the Mystic Shrine, an American order which is restricted to men who have reached the highest degree of the Scottish Rite or who belong to the Knights Templar.

Slinking. A term used in the event of someone being admitted to an Order in which he has no right to be a member.

Steward. The lodge official responsible for ensuring the festive board is well supplied and feasts well catered for.

Tracing Board. The board (also called a trestle board) on which an architect or master builder drew the ground plans for the building to be constructed, which have become pictorial and symbolic representations of the principles pertaining to a particular degree.

Tyler. The lodge officer who guards the door from the outside.

Volume of Sacred Law. The book which is sacred to the religion to which members of a lodge subscribe. Originally the Bible, 'the great light which is from on high', but since shortly after the formation of the United Grand Lodge in 1813 it can now be any recognized sacred text.

Warden. One of the two principal officers of the lodge who rank immediately below the Master in authority. The Senior Warden outranks the Warden.

Working Tools. The square, level, plumb and other tools of the operative mason which now have symbolic meaning to the Freemason and remind him of the principles of his Craft.

York Rite. Descended from the assembly of masons summoned to York by Prince Edwin in AD926, the American system that encompasses the Knights Templar, Royal Arch, Mark Masonry and other Orders.

INDEX

A

Abiff, Hiram 10-11, 16, 20, 112, 114
African countries 76
Ahiman Rezon or a Help to a Brother 57
Aitchison Lodge 36
Aldrin, Edwin 'Buzz' 129
Allende, Salvador 129
American colonies 83-5
American Declaration of
Independence 83, 87-9
Ancient and Accepted (Scottish) Rite
69, 96-7
Ancient Order of Nobles of the Mystic
Shrine 97
Anderson, James 39, 41, 42, 47, 83
anti-Freemasonry measures 61-3, 66,
73-4, 78, 95
anti-Semitism 58
Apartheid 81
Appleton, Sir Edward 130
Arc de Triomphe 121-2
Armstrong, Louis 'Satchmo' 130-1
Arne, Thomas 130
Articles of Union 1813: 58
arts and masons 124-5
Ashbee, Charles 130
Ashmole, Elias 45-6
assembly of lodges 39
Astor, John Jacob 131
Athelstane, King 24, 31
Aubrey, John 20
Audobon, John James 131
Australia 78, 80
Austria 63-4, 73, 125

B

Banks, Sir Joseph 131
Banqueting Hall 44
Bartholdi, Frederic 131
Belcher, Jonathan 83
Berlin, Irving 131
Besant, Annie 136
Beswicke-Royds Manuscript 33
Bolivar, Simón 80-1, 131
Boston Tea Party 86-7
Boswell, James 44, 54
'box clubs' 14
Boyne, Battle of the 56
Bonoparte, Napoleon 71
Burke, Edmund 131
Burns, George 77
Burns, Robert 131

C

Caine, Michael 131
Canada 98-9
candidates procedure 50, 52
Capitol Building, Washington DC 83,
90, 123
cathedral building 23-41
cayennes 27
Central America 82
certificate of membership 103
Chartres Cathedral 29-30
Churchill, Sir Winston 133
coffee houses 50
Collegia 14
Colonies of European Powers 75-6
Comacine Masters 15
Compagnonnage 15, 16
Companions of the Tour of France 27
Conan Doyle, Sir Arthur 133
Constitutions 41, 42, 47, 85
craft guilds 15, 17, 35-6
Craft, The 7, 35
Culloden, Battle of 54
Czechoslovakia 73

D

Daughters of the Nile 98, 137
de Beauharnais, Josephine 71, 134
de Payens, Hugues 13, 17
de Seingalt, G J Casanova 133
Dead Sea Scrolls 13
Degrees
    1st 52, 109-10
    2nd 52, 110-12
    3rd 52, 112-15, 116
    4th-33rd in Scottish Rite 96-7
    33rd 68-9
    Apprentice 109-10
    Fellow Craft 110-12
    Holy Royal Arch 115
    Master Mason 112-15, 116
    Royal Arch 98
    tools representing 52, 109-10
Dempsey, Jack 133
Dermott, Laurence 57, 58
Desaguliers, Theophilus 47-8, 52
Desraimes, Maria 136
Director of Ceremonies 53
Dotzinger, Jost 24, 31
drawing the lodge 50
Droit Humain Lodge, Le 136
Druids 16

Dyer, Colin 46

E

Edward VII, King 63, 133
Edward VIII, King 133
Edwin, Prince 31, 97
Egypt 76
Essenes 16

F

famous freemasons 7, 129-33
famous masons 88
Five Virtues 45, 81, 126-7
Flatiron Building, New York 123
Four Crowned Martyrs 28
France
    apprentice ceremony 104
    Committee of Public Safety 57
    French Revolution 57-8, 59
    Master ceremony 108
    Scottish links 69
    swearing the Oath 104-5
    The Craft 66-9
    Unlawful Societies Act 1799: 58
    women 68, 117, 134-6
Franklin, Benjamin 83-5
Frederick the Great, King of Prussia
65-6
'free' masons 38
*Freemasonry: A Journey Through Ritual
and Symbol* 46-7, 110
Freemasons' Hall 44-5, 120, 121
freestone 38
French Revolution 69-71
fundamental values 27

G

Gambia 76
George IV, King 133
German States 65
Germany and Nazi persecution 73-4
glossary 138-41
Goose and Gridiron Lodge 7, 42, 47
Grand Feast 47-9
Grand Lodges
    African 95
    Antients, The 56-7, 58
    Australia 78, 80
    Canada 98
    Dublin 54, 55
    England 47-9
    France 66, 69, 72

France Woman's 117
Germany 74
Grand Chapter 121
Grand Committee 56
Grand Masters 49
Moderns 57, 58
Munster 54
New Zealand 80
Premier 47
Prince Hall 95
Provincial 53-4
Scotland 54, 55
South Africa 81
Strasbourg 27
Sweden 63
Ulster 54-5
United Grand Lodge of England
54, 58, 103
USA States 89
York 49
Grand Mistress of the St Caroline
Lodge of Adoption 71
Grand Orient, The 69-70, 72, 76
Grand Temple 121
Grande Loge Anglais, La 66

H
Hancock, John 88
Hermetic tradition 47
Higden, Ranulf 9-10
Hogarth, William 48-9
Honourable Fraternity of Ancient
Freemasonry 136
Hull, Richard 76
Hungary 73

I
Illuminati 125
Illustrations of Masonry 57
India 76-8
initiation ceremonies, Knights
Templar 20
Inquisition 62
Islamic fundamentalists 76

J
James II, King 46, 54, 60-1
James VI, King 42
John of Gloucester 37
Jones, Inigo 44-5

K
Kabbalistic tradition 47
Kent, Duke of 7
Kilwinning Lodges 39, 44, 54

King's College Cambridge 40-1
Kipling, Rudyard 78, 79
Knights Templar 13, 16-20, 68, 81

L
L'Innocent Lodge 63
layer 38
Leopold II, Emperor of Austria and
King of Bohemia 125-6
Livingston, Robert 85
Livre de Compagnonnage 15
lodges
current symbolic purpose 27
main titles 27
masons workplaces 24
medieval 36-7
meetings 107-9
military 85
officers 104-6
rites and rituals 101-2
shape 102
Lodges of Adoption 68
London Company of Freemasons 42
Louis XV, King of France 66
Louis XVI, King of France 69-70

M
Magic Flute, The 64, 124-7
Mainwairing, Henry 46
Mark Masonry 116
mark of provenance 30
Martel, Charles 15
Mary Chapel Lodge 42, 44, 54
mason's marks 30-1
masonic buildings 118-22
Masonic Memorial Shrine 121
masons
accepted 44-6, 46
apprentices 27, 36
cowan 38-9
elective 34
fellows 36
'free' 38
honorary members 45
Mark Masons 116
Master Mason 37-8
non-operative 45
operative 34-5
roughe 41
speculative 46,47
vassal 38
Warden 36-7
Master's mark 30
Maximilian, Emperor 24
McNulty, W Kirk 46-7, 110

military lodges 84
Millar, David C 92
miracle plays 35-6
Mithras 13-14
Mopses, Order of 134
moral code 58
Morgan, William 92, 94-5
Mormons 95
Morris, Robert 134, 137, 139
Mother Lodge, The 78
Mozart, W A 64, 124-7

N
Napoleon III, Emperor 71-2
Nebuchadrezzar 42-3
Netherlands 61
non-Christians 58
Norman Conquest 34
Notre Dame Cathedral 23
numbers, Pythagorean science of 12

O
Old Charges 31-3, 39, 47
Orange lodges 55-6
Order of de Molay 137
Order of Job's Daughters 137
Order of the Eastern Star 98, 139
Order of the Rainbow 137
origins of Freemasonry 9-22

P
Paine, Tom 87
Pandects of Amalfi 23
Payne, George 47
Perdiguer, Agricol 15
Philip IV the Fair, King of France 19
pieceworker's mark 30
Pike, Albert 97
Pope, Alexander 48
Popes
Benedict XIV 62
Clement XII 62
Melchiades 28
Portugal 73
positioning mark 30
Preston, William 57
Prince Hall Masonry 95-6
principles 7
Pythagoras 11

Q
Quatour Coronati 28

R
Raffles, Thomas Stamford 78

Ramsay Orations 69
Ratisbon, Statutes of 24-7, 30
regalia 115-18
religious tolerance 57
Revere, Paul 88
rites and rituals 101-2
rituals central to movement 58
Robert the Bruce 19
robes 116-18
Roman Catholic Cathedral, Baltimore 123
Romania 73
Rosicrucians 20-1
Rosse, Earl of 54
Rosslyn Chapel 19-20, 54
Royal Arch Degree 98, 115
Royal Arch Widows 137
Royal Order of Herodem 44
Royal Society 47
Russia 73

S
'Sacred Word' 12-13
St Andrew's Boston Lodge 88
St Barbara 28
St Clair, William 54
St Leger, Elizabeth 134
St Michael, Statutes of 24, 27
St Paul's Cathedral 118
Sayer, Anthony 7, 47
Schaw, William 42, 44
Scotland
    early lodges 36, 44
    French links 69
    Indian links 77

Scottish Rite 69, 96-7
secret signs 35
Sherman, Roger 85
Shriners 97
sign of Honour 31
signs of recognition 30-1
Singapore 78
Solomon's temple, King 10, 20
South America 80-2
Spain 62-3
St John's Philadelphia Lodge 83
Statue of Liberty 90-3
Statute of Labourers 1350: 41
Strasbourg Cathedral 31
Strasbourg, Orders of 30
Stuart, Charles Edward 54
'Supreme Being' 20
Supreme Royal Arch Chapter 100
suspicions of Freemasonry 61
Sussex, Augustus Frederick, Duke of 54-5, 58
Sweden 63
Swift, Jonathan 48
symbolic meaning of offices 106
symbols
    lodges 119
    pillars 20, 119
    Rosslyn Chapel 20
    three banes of life 11

T
Taiwan 78
Timor 74-5
Tracing Boards 118
travelling architects 22

U
Ukraine 73
United States Presidents 90

V
Vale Royal abbey 36

W
Warrington Lodge 46
Washington, George 4, 89-90
Westminster Hall 37
William IV, King 133
William the Conqueror, King 34
women
    Besant, Annie 136
    de Beauharnais, Josephine 71, 135
    Europe 134
    France 68, 117, 134-136
    United Kingdom 134, 136
    United States 97, 134, 137

Y
York Rite 31, 97

Z
Zauberflöte, Die 64, 125-7

PICTURE CREDITS

Akg-images – pp 39, 43, 127

The Art Archive – pp 8, 10, 15, 22, 26, 29, 53, 59, 60, 62, 64, 65, 70-1, 74-5, 80, 86-7, 96, 99, 100, 104-5, 111, 112-3, 119, 122, 124, 125, 135

Bridgeman Art Library – pp 2, 19, 50

Corbis – pp 6, 18, 41, 44, 67, 77, 82, 93, 110, 117, 123, 137

Getty Images – pp 73, 85, 88-9, 128, 130, 131

Mary Evans Picture Library – pp 12, 14, 17, 34, 35, 37, 40, 45, 47, 48-9, 51, 52, 55, 56, 63, 68-9, 72, 79 , 91, 94, 103, 106-7, 108, 115, 117120, 132, 136

Topfoto – pp 21, 25